Craigflower Country

A History of View Royal
1850 – 1950

Edited by

Maureen Duffus

Canadian Cataloguing in Publication Data
Main entry under title:
Craigflower country

Includes bibliographical references and index.
ISBN 1-895332-08-7

1.   View Royal (B.C.)--History.   2.   Hudson's Bay
Company--History.   I. Duffus, Maureen.
FC3849.V53C72 1993   971,1'28   C93-091788-X
F1089.5.V62C72 1993

Financially assisted by:

Health and Welfare Canada New Horizons program (opinions in this publication are not necessarily those of Health and Welfare Canada)

and

The Ministry of Culture through the British Columbia Heritage Trust.

* * * * * *

The View Royal Historical Committee gratefully acknowledges financial assistance from the Town of View Royal, from community business and private donors including PetroCanada, the View Royal Library Association, Meryl Campbell, John Bryant, Richard Rant, Michael Pope, John and Barbara Munton and Ann and Henry Louie.

Designed and typeset in Ventura Publisher 4.1 by
    Desktop Publishing Ltd.
    2604 Quadra St.
    Victoria, B.C.
    V8T 4E4

Printed and bound by:
    Fleming Printing
    200 Esquimalt Road
    Victoria, B.C.
    V9A 3K9

Table of Contents

Acknowledgements

This book has been a community project with contributions from a large number of people, some who wrote chapters for Part II and many who helped in other ways. These include:

- The View Royal Historical Committee which was formed to organize funding and shepherd the project through to publication.

- The contributors who took the time to tell stories of the old days. (Facts have been checked as carefully as possible, but memories of events of half a century or more ago differ.)

- Students of Shoreline Community School who contributed taped interviews conducted on special assignment in 1990.

Special thanks also to the following:

The Mayor and Council of View Royal and staff for their support: Esquimalt Archives volunteers and archivist Marlene Smith; John Adams and staff of B.C. Heritage Properties for access to Craigflower and Cole Island research material; the Naval Museum at HMCS Naden and curator Anne Bissel; the View Royal Library Association; Strawberry Vale Community Club historian Dick Moyer; researcher Trevor Smith for sharing some of his finds from uncatalogued archives material; all who lent photographs from private collections; Michael Pope who copied and catalogued dozens of faded snapshots; photographers Bill John and Rob Duffus for finding old negatives; Dale Mumford of Parks Canada (Fort Rodd Hill) for Cole Island photos; Ray Wunderlich of the Greater Victoria School Board archives who found a a rare photo of the second Craigflower School; Don MacLachlan for E.&N. Railway memorabilia and photos; Canadiana Costume Museum members for dating photographs; staff of the B.C. Archives and Records Service for patience and assistance with research; Gladys Durrant for architectural drawings; Steve Kergin for maps; Bruce Lowther for copy editing and encouragement; Heather West and Russ Malcolm of the B.C. Surveyor General's branch for much valuable information and early maps; Jim Bisakowski, Lee Gabel and Janice Parker at Desktop Publishing, and Mr. Lynn Dunn of Shoreline School for sending students out with tape recorders for interviews that spurred the rest of us to complete a project that had been simmering for years.

For permission to use exerpts from previously published material thanks to: The Women's Canadian Club of Victoria for quotes from *Pioneer Women of Vancouver Island*; T. W. Patterson; St. Columba Church records; the Capital Regional District heritage publications.

Members of the View Royal Historical Committee are: Joe Baur and Michael Pope, editorial board; Allan Murray, chairman; Lloyd Brooks, secretary; Barbara Munton, treasurer; Rossalea Crowe and John Bryant, community liaison; Garry and Betty Chater, research and photography; Louise Baur and Edna Brooks, research assistants; Phyllis McAdams, writer, and John Duffus, critic-at-large.

Craigflower Country

A History of View Royal

1850 – 1950

Parson's Bridge - Esquimalt B.C.

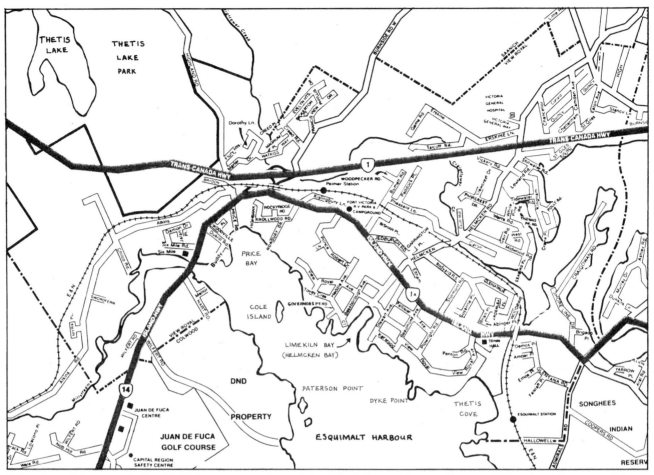

View Royal is one of the 11 little towns and municipalities that make up Greater Victoria. (Courtesy Victoria Street Map Book)

Other Maps:

Introduction

View Royal, formerly known as the Craigflower Country, was once an important part of the much larger Esquimalt District. It is an odd little piece of geography surrounded by four other municipalities and a lot of water. The shoreline includes numerous bays, coves, rocks and beaches of Esquimalt Harbour and the upper reaches of the Gorge, a salt water fiord running inland from Victoria Harbour.

Chief Factor James Douglas of the Hudson's Bay Company bought the place in 1850 from two Songhees Indian groups, the Kosampson and Whyomilth families. He reserved large tracts for Hudson's Bay Company use, including the sawmill site at the head of the harbour (already in operation before the purchase) and two company farms.

The town is sliced into three parts by two major highways which transport thousands daily on their way to somewhere else, and two historic railways, one endangered, the other abandoned. Within the new town, incorporated in 1988 after being an 'unorganized' district for all of its early life, are:

- The remains of a 19th century Hudson's Bay Company farm.

- Two celebrated roadhouses.

- A rapidly growing bedroom community for Victoria.

- A substantial group of residents fighting fiercely to preserve what's left of the rural 'ambience.'

- Thetis Lake and its surrounding forest, which is within the political boundaries but doesn't belong to the town.

There is as yet no town centre, although the part of the Old Island Highway, once lined with 1930s-era motels, is now a commercial strip singularly lacking in charm. The town's heaviest industry is a tent and awning establishment, and there is a slaughterhouse hidden between the two highways. Smoke and smells from a forest products plant on the southeast border sometimes encroach, but on the whole View Royal is spared the afflictions of industry.

In the nineteenth century View Royal was, comparatively, a hive of industry. Sawmills, brick works, lime kilns and railway construction camps sprang up in the the Parson's Bridge area. These and the role of the Hudson's Bay Company in early settlement are the subject of Part I.

Essays in Part II were selected to portray View Royal as it was in the quiet times before it was discovered by developers in the 1960s, and before the rest of Victoria got to know it as the bottleneck responsible for the infamous Colwood Crawl of commuters to and from Victoria.

New political boundaries have been disregarded in some chapters because Craigflower School, Cole Island and other adjacent sites were part of the memories of View Royal children for more than a century. Two Indian reserves and several little islands were also part of the old unorganized district until 1988.

A note about names

Low tide near where Millstream enters Esquimalt Harbour where "shoaling waters" may have given rise to the theory of the meaning of the name Esquimalt.

Esquimalt, pronounced with the accent on 'i' as in eye, is said to have been a Songhees word meaning 'place of shoaling waters.' It is now thought to be the European attempt to pronounce Whyomilth, a family group who had camps and fortifications around Esquimalt Harbour.

View Royal was the name of the 1912 subdivision whose promoters claimed the waterfront lots had "a royal view."

Highway 1A was first known as the Sooke Road and is still commonly called the Old Island Highway.

The Gorge used to be called The Arm, Camosun Arm or Victoria Arm. The present name used to refer only to the reversing falls where the tidal inlet narrows at Tillicum Road.

When the Gorge widens into a large basin beyond Craigflower Bridge it is called Portage Inlet because the narrow neck of land between it and Esquimalt Harbour used to be a canoe portage.

Christie Point, the long peninsula jutting into Portage Inlet, was known as The Pie until John Christie bought the Craigflower property in 1936.

Cole Island was known locally as Magazine Island.

Deadman's Creek is now called Craigflower Creek by newcomers and mapmakers.

Limekiln Cove and Helmcken Bay are one and the same.

The Puget's Sound Agricultural Company was a division of the Hudson's Bay Company. It is often referred to as the Puget Sound Company in later writings. PSAC is simpler.

The Mill Farm, Esquimalt Farm and Colwood Farm are one and the same. Captain Edward Edwards Langford's domain covered parts of View Royal, Langford and Colwood.

Millstream was originally called Rowe's Stream, named after Thomas Rowe, paymaster of the survey ship HMS Fisgard.

The First Inhabitants

Apart from a short visit by a boatload of Spanish sailors in 1792, and occasional skirmishes with marauding native enemies from the north, the Indians of Esquimalt Harbour and Portage Inlet had forest and shore to themselves until 1843. In 1850 the Kosampson and Whyomilth groups signed the Douglas Treaties selling land which included all present day View Royal.

As Chief Andy Thomas, a descendant of one of the Kosampson people who signed the treaty, says, most histories write about First Nations people in the past tense, as if they no longer existed. They are here, on the Esquimalt and Songhees reserves which were once part of View Royal. They are writing their own story. The following chapter takes a short look at the more distant past.[1]

Feasts and Fortifications

Joe Baur

Evidence of Indian habitation along the View Royal shores is found in a number of small sites, mainly in the upper reaches of the harbour and in the Christie Point area of Portage Inlet. Some may have been permanent sites occupied by small groups or seasonal camps used as living requirements dictated.

Shoreline midden sites abound in the area. There is evidence on Richards and Cole islands that many seafood feasts took place there. Most archaeological sites date to between 100 and 200 years ago, but one site in the Parson's Bridge area appears to be about 800 years

old. It is possible older sites will be unearthed in View Royal adjacent to the Maple Bank site which is nearly 2,000 years old. The nearby south Gorge Bridge midden is 4,000 years old.

There are signs of Indian earthworks at the foot of Stewart Avenue where the shore forms a promontory with sheer rock cliffs to the water, affording a natural defence from waterborn invasion while leaving only the neck of land unprotected.

The inhabitants seem to have dug a deep straight-sided ditch across the neck of land, making attacks

---

1   According to a census taken by James Douglas at about the time he signed treaties with the Kosampson and Whyomilth families in 1850, the 105-member Kosampson group had 21 bearded men, 23 women, 35 boys and 26 girls. The Whyomilth group had 18 bearded men, 20 women, 36 boys and 39 girls. Wilson Duff in his B.C. Studies paper *The Fort Victoria Treaties*, Fall, 1969 explains: "Native people of Victoria who came to be known collectively as the 'songish' or 'Songhees,' were never in any political sense a single tribe. They were comprised of a large number of more or less automonous household groups, whose sprawling plank houses were clustered in a number of winter villages, and who moved regularly from place to place in the course of their annual round of activities" (Page 23)

from that direction difficult. To add to this inhospitable bulwark a palisade of sharpened poles was thought to have been set into the ground, positioned to impale any invader emerging from the ditch. Members of the band living outside the stockade would be summoned to take up positions within the protected area at the first sign of possible attack.

When there was a threat of imminent attack from warlike tribes from northern Vancouver Island the natives living on Songhees Point, in Victoria Harbour, would retreat up the Gorge waterway to seek refuge and a safe haven in the View Royal area. They would camp where the Gorge waterway meets Portage Inlet, near the site of the original Craigflower School. If the attackers pursued, the Songhees people would make their stand at the narrow passage of water now spanned by Craigflower Bridge.

Although this area was within Kosampson territory, and the village of Sahsum was situated at the north end of the bridge, the Songhees appeared to be welcome visitors and perhaps were even permitted to use the great earthwork that had been erected by the Sahsums. This earthwork, which was destroyed when the new Craigflower schoolyard was extended south toward the shore, was constructed by moving soil from a large area of shoreline to create a great knoll. It was used as a lookout station to warn the natives in the village of a possible enemy attack. This huge dais was also used for ceremonial purposes and celebrations. The Kosampson people once again became View Royal's close neighbours in 1843 when they moved to the village of Kala, situated on Esquimalt Harbour at View Royal's southern border.

Numerous individual burial sites have been discovered, most of them along the Prince Robert Ridge. Bodies were buried in rock crevices, probably to prevent disturbance by animals. There is some indication of attempts at tree burials near Erskine Lane, but this type of burial did not appear to be suitable for the area. As one oldtimer said, "whenever you walked underneath the trees little bits would drop on you." There are more sites to be investigated, but most are on private land.

Southern Vancouver Island chiefs were photographed in ceremonial dress for the 1927 visit of the governor general of Canada, Viscount Willingdon, who was made an honorary chief of the Kosampson (Sahsum) tribe. Among the chiefs in the picture are David LaTasse, second from right with spear and fur hat, and at his right Chief Michael Cooper of the Songhees who presented an "Indian walking stick" to the governor general. (RBCM 16761)

The Nineteenth Century

Maureen Duffus

The Hudson's Bay Company, the Royal Navy and other early landowners

Cole Island.

Craigflower farmhouse.

Some Important Dates

When the first Europeans came to what is now View Royal the main action was at Fort Victoria, four miles to the east by trail or waterway. Early activity around Esquimalt Harbour was all directly related to the Hudson's Bay Company and its officers. Nearly all the first landowners were, or had been, HBC employees. The following outline of contemporary events gives some background to early development west of the fort.

1837: Captain William Henry McNeill on the HBC steamship *Beaver* explores the southern part of Vancouver Island as a possible site for a new company headquarters, and recommends it.

1842-43: James Douglas chooses Victoria Harbour rather than Esquimalt Harbour as the site for the new fur trade post. Work begins. Douglas returns to Fort Vancouver in the Oregon Territory.

1846: First hydrographic surveys of Esquimalt Harbour begin. Royal Navy officers give their names to View Royal islands, points and coves.

1848: Roderick Finlayson, in charge of Fort Victoria, orders construction of a sawmill at Rowe's Stream, probably the first European structure in Esquimalt Harbour.

1849: Hudson's Bay Company acquires Vancouver Island lease at seven shillings a year.

Chief Factor Douglas returns to take charge. First Scots immigrants arrive.

1850: Governor Richard Blanshard, 32-year-old Oxford-educated barrister, arrives March 11 to a cool reception from fur trade officials.

Company doctor John Sebastian Helmcken arrives at Esquimalt March 24 and takes a fancy to some land across the harbour. William Richard Parson, millwright, arrives to take charge of the sawmill and grist mill.

New machinery for the grist mill arrives on the same ship.

James Douglas completes purchase of land from the Kosampson and Whyomilth families.

1851: Disillusioned Governor Blanshard leaves. Chief Factor James Douglas is appointed to replace him.

Captain James Cooper returns on the *Tory* as an independent settler.

Captain Edward Edwards Langford and family arrive on the same ship with small labour force for the company farm at the end of Esquimalt Harbour.

Dr. Helmcken purchases Section VIII, now, central View Royal, on December 15.

1852: Chief Factor/Governor Douglas, acting as land agent for the British government, sells more land to settlers after reserving choice land for Company farms, and for schools, churches and public buildings for the new colony.

Captain Cooper puts a down payment on Section III, next to land that will become Craigflower farm.

1853: Kenneth McKenzie and party arrive to begin work at the Maple Point farm, soon known as Craigflower, the largest of the four Puget's Sound Agricultural Company farms.

Various carpenters and labourers arrive with him to serve out their five-year contracts as company employees. Hostility between the Company and the 'lower orders' increases.

1854: William Richard Parson, Company millwright, acquires 39 acres "abutting upon the northernmost part of Esquimalt Harbour."

1855: Classes begin at newly-built Craigflower Schoolhouse

1856: Richard Parson pays £75 for a retail liquor licence for his hotel at Parson's Bridge.

James Stewart builds his farmhouse on land leased from Dr. Helmcken between the Four Mile Hill and Parson's Bridge.

1857: Several Craigflower servants claim land promised on completion of their contracts with the company.

1858: Former Craigflower employee Peter Calvert and bride move to their new home on the Four Mile Hill, soon to become an inn.

1862: Cole Island is cleared for construction of a naval powder magazine.

1885: Construction of E.&N. Railway starts in View Royal.

1912: Dr. James Douglas Helmcken sells part of Helmcken property to the Island Investment Company for subdivision.

With the subdivision of the old Stewart farm View Royal begins its slow, uneven growth as a bedroom suburb of Victoria.

Aerial photo of Cole Island. (Michael Pope collection)

The Earliest Landowners

The first European landlord was the Hudson's Bay Company. With a firm foothold at Fort Victoria since 1843, company directors convinced Her Majesty's Government that its men on the spot were best qualified to rule Vancouver Island. Despite considerable opposition in London they managed to lease the whole Island for seven shillings a year. This controversial arrangement lasted from 1849 to 1858.

The Company, in the person of James Douglas acting as land agent for the first few years, sold some land to a few independent settlers. But large tracts were kept in the company reserve, including the sawmill site at Rowe's Stream and land for the Company farms at Maple Point (Craigflower) and at the head of Esquimalt Harbour (Mill Farm, later known as Esquimalt Farm or Colwood).

The first individual land purchasers were the fort doctor John Sebastian Helmcken, former Company ship captain James Cooper and former Company millwright William Richard Parson. Between them, by 1855, they owned all but two sections of the land between Craigflower Farm and the Company millsite, from the north shore of Esquimalt Harbour to Deadman's Creek and beyond.[2]

Parson, millwright at the ill-fated water-driven mill, bought land near the mill site and opened a roadhouse in 1855 on the site of the present Six Mile House Hotel. Peter Calvert, late of Craigflower Farm, acquired six acres of Cooper's land and set up as an innkeeper at the Four Mile House. By 1858 Helmcken was the largest landowner but leased a large part of his property to James Stewart and family until this section was sold for subdivision in 1912.

These and other people who farmed the land were major players in the early history of View Royal.

---

2 Original dates are different to establish. Douglas as land agent wrote to headquarters in January, 1851, for the forms for land titles as, quite sensibly, the would-be purchasers "object to paying for the lots they wish to take, until they receive titles." Again in April he begs for even a simple "printed form of title, filled in here..." Some handwritten agreements of sale signed by Douglas give definite dates, but many official records for the Helmcken, Cooper and Parson purchases are dated October 8, 1855. Originals are held by the B.C. Surveyor General.

The Mill at Rowe Stream

Land ownership was not a major consideration in 1847 when a party of Indians led Roderick Finlayson to the head of Esquimalt for his first look at a freshwater stream with a waterfall. What the Hudson's Bay Company wanted it took, and what it desperately wanted was a sawmill. All company establishments needed lumber for building and for sale if possible. As early as 1843 James Douglas informed London headquarters that the reversing falls at the Gorge might supply the necessary power.

He thought a sawmill or flour mill could be erected "on the canal of Camosack at a point where the channel is contracted to a breadth of 47 feet by two narrow ridges of granite projecting from either bank into the canal, through which the tide rushes out and in with a degree of force and velocity capable of driving the most powerful machinery, if guided and applied by mechanical skill."

The letter continues "I mentioned ... that I proposed to erect any machinery required for the establishment at the narrows of this canal, where there is a boundless

Thirty-year-old Roderick Finlayson, who was senior officer at Fort Victoria until James Douglas arrived to take permanent charge in 1849, was responsible for construction of the saw mill and grist mill at the waterfall where Millstream enters Esquimalt Harbour. (BCARS 4750)

water power, which our two millwrights, Crate and Fenton, think might, at a moderate expense, be applied to that object. A fresh-water river would certainly be in many respects more convenient, as the moving power could be made to act with greater regularity, and be applied to machinery at probably less labour and expense than a tide power."[3]

Alas. The waterfall that Finlayson saw on his first visit on August 4, 1847, was at its roaring best after heavy summer rain. But it turned out to be a most unreliable fall, requiring great labour and expense over its short, troublesome life span.[4]

The mill at Rowe Stream was the earliest European building in Esquimalt Harbour, predating the first naval buildings at the entrance to the harbour by eight years. Finlayson records his frequent visits to the mill site, either riding or walking the six miles over his new road, or by canoe.

Of his August, 1847, expedition he wrote: "Proceeded direct to Esquimalt Bay to examine a stream of fresh water, reported by Indians to be there & found it as re-

---

3 Cited in W. Kaye Lamb, *Early Lumbering on Vancouver Island*, B.C. Historical Quarterly, v.ii.
4 Details of construction of the sawmill and grist mill and their problems are from *The Fort Victoria Post Journal, 1846 to 1851*, H.B.C. Archives, University of Manitoba.

ported, running over a ledge of rocks, the site being apparently well adapted for a mill."

"Apparently" is the operative word. The falls are a glorious sight in full spate, a gentle trickle in dry weather - in fact most of the year. But Finlayson had little choice. The nearest reliable source of water power was 20 miles away at Sooke, too far away from the fort to be any use.[5]

Five months passed before the short-staffed company officer began work on a road from the fort to the mill site. The journal entry for January 17, 1848, relates that "... Mr. Niven and myself started with 8 hands and as many Indians to cut the road to the Mill seat, from the plains through the wood to the rapid in Concordia Arm [the Gorge] to bridge that place." Two days later he marked the route "from the fall to the

mill seat" and had men "squaring wood for the bridge, cutting out the road to the mill seat."[6]

A dwelling house was built for Mr. Niven's work party which now included two French deserters from a whaling ship. The first timbers were raised on April 1 with the help of oxen not needed elsewhere.

Mr. Fenton, the first millwright, arrived from Fort Nisqually, near present day Tacoma, Washington, to supervise the party of French Canadians, Indians and Kanakas (Hawaiians), most of whom came down with measles which was raging through the fort and Indian village in epidemic proportions.

The foundations of the water wheel, the shaft and cogs were prepared in June and the dwelling house was moved, " ... the former site having been too near the saw mill."

The reversing falls at the Gorge narrows where Douglas first proposed building a sawmill. The bridge was part of Roderick Finlayson's road to the mill at the head of Esquimalt Harbour, and consisted of "five large logs placed across the fall in Concordia Arm at which seven hands were employed for the last eight days."On February 2, 1848, Finlayson reported the bridge completed and "rode across it this morning on horseback." (BCARS 8049, ca. 1860)

The mill was ready to go in September, but the wheel stood still. Finlayson and Fenton undertook a two-day expedition "up the country above Esquimalt" to look for other streams which might be diverted into the mill stream - Fenton's enthusiastic first impression of the fall having been overly optimistic.

They walked and climbed through "the most rugged and forbidding country imaginable," climbed what is now Mount Finlayson for "a splendid view of the surrounding country" and probably the first European sight of Finlayson Arm, "... an arm of the sea which extends to a distance of about 10 miles from the sea and the sanetch village." They had high hopes when they found a large lake

---

5   A water driven sawmill was in operation in 1849 when Victoria's first settler, Captain Walter Colquhoun Grant, tried his hand as a colonist at Sooke. The mill was later run profitably by members of the Muir family.

6   His approximate route would have been north from the Fort, west along the Gorge, possibly as far back as Burnside Road, crossing the Gorge at Tillicum, along Craigflower Road and through View Royal to Parson's Bridge, then to the head of the harbour.

There is still a deep pool at the head of the Millstream falls where the water was dammed in an attempt to keep the mill working. A narrow water course to the right of the main falls appears to have been cut for extra power.

(almost certainly Thetis Lake) which might empty into the lagoon where a mill could be "made to work every day of the year." Hopes were dashed. They found that the lake seeped into swamps which went nowhere.

Fenton also "examined the stream at the head of Camosun Arm and found water in it not sufficient to drive a grist mill." This was most likely Deadman's (or Craigflower) Creek running into Portage Inlet.

Finlayson had no choice. HBC workers could not be left to idle about. Four extra men and 10 Indians were sent out on October 23, 1848, to raise the beams and posts of the grist mill below the sawmill.

Next day Finlayson took Douglas, who was on a visit from Fort Vancouver, to inspect the unproductive mill. The journal does not record the chief factor's comments.

Finally, the heavy west coast rains came and the stream winding down from a lake in the Highlands filled to overflowing. On Friday November 24, 1848, the machinery clanked into action for the first time. Finlayson's journal entry is brief, noting simply that "...The Indians who came today for the mill rations brought a line from Mr. Fenton reporting that he got the saw mill at length under way ..." Less than a week later he recorded the first of a series of mishaps to the mill machinery.

A pile of rocks is all that remains of the foundations of the grist mill. The location was confirmed by the owner of the site who remembers that timbers still stood on the crumbling foundation in the 1920s. (Maureen Duffus photos)

Mill For Sale

The mill site was included in an early attempt to sell the Hudson's Bay Company's Colwood Farm, begun in 1851 under the erratic management of Captain Edward Edwards Langford. The following advertisement appeared in the Colonist of February 19, 1859, shortly after Langford had been dismissed for his extravagance and the general aggravation he caused almost from the day of his arrival.

385 ACRES "NEAR MOUTH OF ESQUIMALT HARBOUR"

VANCOUVER'S ISLAND - FOR SALE

*A farm of 385 acres of the richest description of arable land, **near the mouth of the important Harbour of Esquimalt**. About 60 acres have been broken and fenced in. A commodious residence, excellent barn, and other outhouses. For a stock farm it is second to none in the country.*

Situated on the coast facing the Olympian range on the opposite shores of the Straits of Fuca, with a road running thro the estate, possesses a good boat harbour, valuable oak and pine timber, a rustling stream and a large water power or mill privilege with from 30 to 40 feet fall.

To anyone wishing to invest in real estate this is a rare opportunity ... immediate possession can be had, with a clear and direct title from the Colonial Government.

FOR SALE also 20 acres of rich bottom land, well watered and finely timbered, in the Salt Lake, one mile outside Esquimalt Harbour.

The above will be sold at Auction entire, or in lots to suit purchasers, at Victoria, VI, on the 28th day of April, 1859, unless previously disposed of by private contract. Apply to Mr. James Cooper, Esquimalt or to HPP Crease Esq. Barrister at Law, VI Selim Franklin &CO, Auctioneers and Land agents.

The Company held the mill site until 1922 when the Pollock Brothers bought the land on both sides of Millstream falls.

" ... Some of the saw mill gearing got deranged in the course of last night." And so it went. Fenton brought the crank to the fort for repair for the first but not the last time. The saw was brought in "considerably bent, some of the iron work binding it having given away, which will stop it for several days." The blacksmith struggled to make new machinery with whatever was at hand. When the machinery was working the stream dried up, and when the water was plentiful the machinery broke down.

Failing machinery was only part of the problem. Four oxen were sent out in January; one "fell into a hole near the mill and was unfortunately killed." When Finlayson visited the mill party he found "the Mill at work but owing to the dry and frosty weather the water is rather scant ... " and only working about two days a week. One of the men "was seriously hurt by a fall in descending the bank before the people's dwelling there."

An early photo shows a naval pinnace getting water at the foot of Millstream Falls, several years before a long flume was built. (BCARS 31320)

The short journal entries suggest a frustrated Finlayson. Just as the new gearing sent from England was ready in March, 1849, he reluctantly gave orders to stop the mill and replace the old machinery, a circumstance " ... which is to be regretted as there is now abundance of water in the mill stream."

He was also concerned when a party of 'Kowitchans' were said to be prowling about the mill "and shortly afterwards the whole of the Songes Camp were under arms in pursuit of them ... " The mill in the woods far away from the fort was not a safe house.

That April Fenton the millwright left for the California gold mines. His successors were George McKenzie, who had "a remarkably handsome half-breed wife, laughing good-natured and industrious," according to Dr. Helmcken, and William Richard Parson.

Despite its continuing problems, the mill did produce lumber. The first is said to have been used for the floor of the granary at the Hudson's Bay Company's North Dairy Farm. On April 27, 1849, a shipment of 8,238 feet was sent to Fort Langley.

Eventually there was enough for export. The first shipment at £80 per 1,000 feet, bound for California, was barged out to the brig *Collooney* anchored across the harbour. Another shipment of 100,000 feet went on the *Cayuga* for California. The captain deposited $7,000 in gold dust as security.

But was the mill ever the profitable enterprise the Company of Gentleman Adventurers hoped for? It was already obsolete by 1853 when a steam sawmill was in operation at Craigflower Farm. Ironically, a flash flood from the normally placid Millstream seriously damaged the machinery in 1854 or '55.

The wheel was replaced and there is some indication that the mill was still running in 1858. The Colonist of July 14, 1858, tells readers of a creek running into Esquimalt Harbour, "whose water power runs a couple of sawmills." Ships were accustomed to get fresh water from the stream, but " ... on a recent occasion the captain of the schooner Alice was denied the privilege of filling his casks from the water that was going to waste by running into the Bay." The Colonist deplores "this dog-in-the-manger action" and trusts it was not authorized by the company. (The *Alice* was brought out from England in sections by Captain James Cooper, a disgruntled former HBC employee.)

A 1940 photograph of Millstream falls shows the pool where sailors filled water barrels. (Pollock collection)

Doctor Helmcken's Fancy

Dr. John Sebastian Helmcken reached Vancouver Island on March 24, 1850, on the Hudson's Bay Company ship *Norman Morison*. The ship was held in quarantine for several days in Esquimalt Harbour because there had been several cases of smallpox on the voyage.

While the rest of the passengers "set to work to scrub their things ... the washing and drying was done near where the Hudson's Bay store and Maple Bank now are" the 26-year-old London doctor explored the countryside from Esquimalt to Langford with the ship's captain, David Durham Wishart. We have his account of these hikes from reminiscences written in the 1890s.[7]

"It was pretty monotonous in quarantine ... the Captain and I used to walk about ... Langford Plains and thereabouts. ... It was an awfully pretty place, covered with grass and wild flowers, and red-winged starling flitted about in the willows - how much land we travelled over there is uncertain, but Wishart had good ideas of locality and we always found our way back - pretty tired sometimes, for there were no trails in the bush then ... the sawmill existed at Rowe's Stream ... "

One of the earliest photographs of the young Fort Victoria doctor John Sebastian Helmcken appears to be taken near the fort palisade, shown faintly in the background. (BCARS 8225)

From the ship the doctor and the captain could go by boat or canoe across the entrance of Esquimalt Harbour to what is now Fort Rodd Hill, then up towards the present Juan de Fuca Recreation Centre. Or they could walk along a trail, later Admirals Road, to Finlayson's road to the mill site, now the Old Island Highway. This route would pass through some of the property Helmcken was to buy the following year.

"The piece of land which my son James now holds took my fancy and I determined to get it somehow or other. At this time a few acres of land seemed to me a big piece - so utterly ignorant was I of land perhaps on account of having been brought up in London. I only applied for twenty acres! Well, £20 pounds was a good sum to me in those days ... "

Eventually Helmcken was to own most of what is now central View Royal, between James Cooper's section and Parson's Bridge, from the shores of Esquimalt Harbour to Burnside Road. Reports of land sales for 1853-60 show that Helmcken purchased Lot 9, Section VIII, Esquimalt District, 53 acres, on December 15, 1851, thus becoming a landowner two years

---

7   All following quotes are from Helmcken's reminiscences in a family collection and from notes to the published work edited by Dorothy Blakey Smith, U.B.C. Press, 1975.

before Craigflower Farm was begun. He continued to buy land for the next decade.

"At this time the Captain and I believed Esquimault to be destined to become a very important place, but neither of us thought anything of Victoria ... " Later in the journal he says that "At this time, every one believed that Esquimault would be the site of the future city. Victoria served very well the purposes of the HB Co and the village, but when the big ships arrived and commerce became great, which every one imagined would be, then Esquimault must necessarily be the place."

By 1892, when he was writing his reminiscences, Helmcken was not so sure the "Esquimault land I bought for my children - for them to have something to live on when they came or grew up" was such a great idea. He is critical of the Hudson's Bay Company's handling of land sales in the 1850s, when "money obtained from the disposal of land was ... deemed sufficient to pay the expense of colonization."

As Helmcken saw it, the Hudson's Bay Company governor and directors in London "seem to have had the English ideas of the value of the soil, when in truth the soil, market &c. bore no resemblance. The land in England was valuable because money had been spent on it to ... make it fit for cultivation and production. Here the case was exactly the opposite - land covered with a dense forest, very difficult to clear - had it been open prairie it could have been sold and settled but naturally people shirked woods and Indians."

He continues: "I paid five dollars per acre for all the land I bought at Esquimault, rocks as well. The Puget's Sound Co did the same - the HBCo held land for about ten miles around Victoria as their right without payment - a sort of possessory claim of the Fur Trade Branch. It was soon found that very little money came in from the sale of land ... Those who

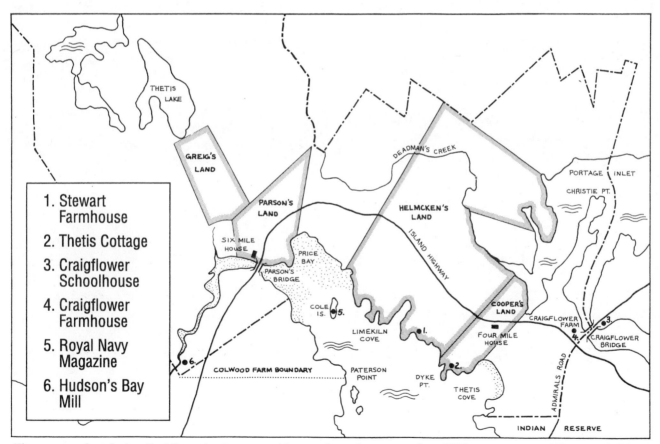

1. Stewart Farmhouse
2. Thetis Cottage
3. Craigflower Schoolhouse
4. Craigflower Farmhouse
5. Royal Navy Magazine
6. Hudson's Bay Mill

The extent of early landholdings is shown on this map based on part of an 1858 survey map of Esquimalt District. (B.C. Surveyor General)

bought did not do so from speculative purposes, but because they wanted land to live on in their old age or to leave farms for their children. No one supposed land to be or likely to become of great value and five dollars was thought exorbitant, particularly when in Washington Territory people could get 640 [acres] for nothing ..."

At any rate sales were so slow the land office, still run by the company, " ... used almost [to] beg some of us to buy, but refusal was general - no one would give five dollars for rocks that were incapable of producing anything."

Eventually London headquarters gave the local land office permission "to sell the land and throw the rocks without payment into the bargain and subsequently swamps went in the same way. ... In this way the rocks and swamps were thrown in and I bought section C under this arrangement." It was, he says, "a derelict piece of land, which no one would look at - and indeed which I knew very little about - but the money was wanted - and the HBCo I presume wanted to show a decent report to HM Govt. This derelict piece of land I have still - and an awful piece it is. A hundred dollars per acre will not make the land ploughable."

Some idea of the state of View Royal before any of the land was cleared for Craigflower Farm is included in Helmcken's grumble about his "worthless" purchase:

"No-one nowadays seems to understand the conditions of the early days - land was worthless and could not be sold and indeed remained so until the gold discoveries and even then there was but little demand - the country so forbidding. Had anyone foreseen the rise of Victoria and the future value of proximate lands, he might have bought the whole country had he the money. The worst of it was - none of us had any money! So we could not indulge much in this even at the time of the excitement [the 1858 gold rush] - save Pemberton and Pearse who chose Victoria for their investment and Yates the Arm. " (J. D. Pemberton and B. Pearse, as land surveyors, had first go at desirable properties, as did HBC officers Roderick Finlayson, John Work, William Fraser Tolmie, John Tod and others.)

There is no record that Helmcken ever lived on the View Royal land but about 50 acres were cleared and made productive after he leased them to the land steward from Craigflower Farm.

The old doctor was still alive when his son, Dr. James Douglas Helmcken, sold 80 acres of his waterfront property to a development company in 1912. And so 'this derelict piece of land' became, according to the developers, "... of a character to charm the most colorless pessimist [rising] from the water almost at the angle of a modern theatre auditorium ... every lot a commanding view of the harbor, the straits and the Olympics ... " How the 'rocks and swamps' were transformed! One of Dr. Helmcken's grandchildren kept his part of the property until 1929, and a great granddaughter remembered in 1992 her childhood there in the 1920s.

The Stewarts Of Seaview Farm

The man who rented the "unploughable" land from Helmcken was listed on the passenger list of the *Norman Morison* 1852-53 voyage as Stewart, James, with wife and infant. They travelled in the intermediate class, between the gentry and the lower orders, as befits a land steward to the farm manager. A native of Haddington, Scotland, James Stewart was recruited by Kenneth McKenzie, and is said to have been one of the few who got along with his employer. His house at Craigflower was across from McKenzie's big house, separated from it by the road to Langford's farm.

After nine years at Craigflower, according to his obituary in the Colonist June 24, 1892, he moved to "a piece of land owned by Dr. Helmcken on Esquimalt Harbour in the year 1862." (This conflicts with the date given by his daughter, who said her father built the farmhouse in 1856. It is believed he stayed at Craigflower at least until 1858 to complete his five-year contract.)

The obituary continues: "Mr. Stewart made no further change of location. Year after year he laboured on, till gradually smiling fields of waving grain took the place of sombre pine." When James died two of his children, John and Amy, continued to farm.

The Amazing 'Aunt Amy'

The last of six children, and only daughter of James and Isabella Stewart, Amy became 'the grand old lady' of View Royal. She was born in 1870 and remembered her early days clearly.

"My father began building our house in 1856, just one year after Craigflower School was opened, from logs hewn out of the forest surrounding us," she recalled in an undated interview. "All the nails and hardware came from Scotland. It consisted of three rooms and only one door that gave entrance or exit to or from the house. In those early days we never knew who might land on the rocky shore in front of our home, and father did not want any doubtful visitor to come sneaking up on us, so the door was all we ever had."

The Stewart farmhouse on Kerwood Road before it was demolished in 1946 by a highways department crew to complete road construction. (Photo courtesy Margaret McIntyre Tront, ca. 1933)

She remembered the Indians who visited constantly to sell their beautiful handiwork for 25 or 50 cents, plus a little salt or soap, and that "they often told us of merchantmen who were trying to escape from their ships by hiding in the forest around our home."

An early picture of Amy and friends. Left to right are Ethel Helmcken, Edith Helmcken, Dorothy McTavish, Amy Stewart and Cecelia Helmcken at the Stewart farmhouse, ca. 1885. (McTavish collection)

A later picture (left) of two of the ladies with their mother taken near the McTavish greenhouses ca. 1905. Seated, centre, is Mrs. G. A. McTavish (Dr. Helmcken's daughter Catherine Amelia) with daughters Dorothy Olivia, later Mrs. Edward Heddle, seated, and Margaret Cecilia (Rita), later Mrs. David Hughes. The boys are unidentified. (From a glass plate negative, McTavish collection)

*Amy Stewart, back row fourth from right, attended Craigflower School from the age of six in 1876, walking from the farm with her older brothers. She treasured a book called **Favorite Narratives of a Christian Household** awarded to her brother John for diligence during the 1863 school year. She was one of the former pupils at the centennial party at the schoohouse in 1958. (BCARS 14374, ca. 1884)*

Portrait of Amy Stewart as a young girl when the Stewart farmhouse saw visiting naval officers, and even Sir James Douglas and his family, as guests. (BCARS 95609)

Royal Navy officers enjoyed the Stewart family hospitality, and the Stewarts visited the ships in return. Amy remembered her father would return with a bundle of Old Country newspapers, and she might be given a sailor's cap with the ship's name on the ribbon. The farm supplied ships with milk, eggs, vegetables and fruit.

After James Stewart died Amy milked her share of cows night and morning, tending the chickens, which she called by name. Her neighbours remember her famous Christmas puddings which she "wouldn't give a hang for without a tot of rum in it." She never boiled a Christmas pudding in the house, declaring it was much better done on a fire in the garden about three weeks before the festive season. She claimed her pet chickens always appreciated the warmth.

When the land was sold for subdivision in 1912 Amy and her brother John bought a double lot on what is now Stewart Avenue. Miss Stewart moved out of the old farmhouse into her new house in 1913 but continued to keep a few Jersey cows until 1943. A niece, Mrs. Lillian Culling, lives in the house now.

Captain Cooper's Ventures

Captain James Cooper, late of the Company's marine division, bought 53 acres of land in View Royal shortly after he returned to Vancouver Island in 1851 as an independent settler.[8] A fellow passenger on the *Tory* was Captain Edward Edwards Langford who brought his fashionable wife and daughters and a small work force for the Company farm he was to manage.

The 30-year-old Cooper also brought his wife, "a very handsome Englishwoman," according to Helmcken, and an iron ship, in sections, which he intended to use for trade with San Fransico and Hawaii. He planned to make a lot of money.

Cooper's many business ventures were highly imaginative, if not entirely successful. His plan to sell Fraser Valley cranberries and potatoes to the San Francisco market was brought to an acrimonious end. The monopolistic Hudson's Bay Company, the only source of barrels for shipping the berries, inexplicably found it necessary to charge $3 for

"A fine-looking florid stout able man, but of an irascible grumbling disposition" is the way his contemporary and sometime political colleague Dr. Helmcken describes James Cooper. "He ought to have been prosperous here but for some reason was not." (BCARS 22755)

barrels worth, according to the indignant Cooper, 30 cents. To Cooper's chagrin the company soon went into the cranberry business itself without the high overhead of pricey barrels.

He prospered briefly as a liquor vendor in Victoria until Governor James Douglas, and compliant members of the Legislative Council, imposed a tax of £120 a year on retail sales of spirits. Surprisingly, Cooper was also a member of the governing council, appointed by former governor Blanshard, but not a Douglas favourite. Somehow a letter from Douglas informing Cooper of the meeting on the tax measure failed to reach Cooper in time for him to attend. Cooper was livid, Douglas was smug. Minutes of the October, 1852, council meeting read:

"That we consider it derogatory to the character of a Member of Council to be a retail dealer in spirituous Liquors, or to follow any calling that may endanger the peace or be injurious to public morals."

Hostility between Cooper and Douglas grew worse after the insubordinate ex-

---

8   Cooper's major landholding was in Metchosin, where Thomas Blinkhorn was in charge of a sizeable farm. The farmhouse on Happy Valley Road was near Bilston Creek, named after the English parish where Cooper was born. The 385 acres included land that is now Witty's Lagoon Regional Park. For more on Cooper's Metchosin Land holdings, see *Footprints*, published by the Metchosin School Museum Society in 1983.

Thetis Cottage, the Coopers' home in View Royal, was in a cleared area at Dyke Point. The white-painted structure is named on early Royal Navy hydrographic charts as a navigation point for ships entering Esquimalt Harbour. Long after the cottage was gone a triangular white-painted wooden marker on the point served the same purpose. From across the harbour the beacon looked vaguely like a crinoline-skirted lady, so the point was known unofficially as White Lady Point. (BCARS 10305)

employee returned to England to testify at Parliamentary hearings in London, carrying with him statements signed by other 'reformers.'[9] In one of his first bursts of investigative journalism, Colonist editor Amor de Cosmos published Cooper's testimony about a mountain of grievances as front page news in 1859.

To the great annoyance of Governor Douglas, ex-Council member Cooper managed to get himself appointed harbour master. Colonial Secretary Sir Edward Bulwer Lytton drew up a civil list for the young colony. Major appointments included Douglas as governor, Matthew Baillie Begbie as judge, Chartres Brew, inspector of police, George Hunter Cary as attorney general - and the tiresome Cooper as harbour master.

The appointment of an old political opponent, who still owed a large debt to the Company store and had yet to complete payment for his land, was not one of HM government's better choices, according to Douglas. He wrote to the Duke of Newcastle, former colonial secretary, that he considered Cooper's office to be "a sinecure," and that its holder had allied himself "with the clique who abuse and vilify the government, through the columns of a newspaper which is called the 'British Colonist,'" for which Cooper was "actually one of the sureties."[10]

By the early 1860s Cooper was back to land speculation. Parts of his View Royal land, Section III on an 1858 map, were surveyed and lots advertised for sale in Cooperville, the first attempt at residential development in View Royal. The plan also shows what was probably the first of many proposals for a canal between Portage Inlet and Esquimalt Harbour.

Part of Cooper's planned subdivision showed lots between the Sooke Road and Dyke Point. The plan was deposited at the BC surveyor general's office by Elizabeth Calvert of the Four Mile House in 1878.

Although the proposed Cooperville never materialized, part of the property bordering on Craigflower Farm was acquired by ex-Craigflower employee Peter Calvert whose new home on the Four Mile Hill soon became a favourite stopping place for travellers to the western farms.

Another buyer was Attorney General George Hunter Cary who owned "3 water lots on Cooper's Estate in Esquimalt District," according to the 1863 voters registration list for Esquimalt District. Lots in a subdivision called Collingwood Estates, where Cooperville was proposed in the 1860s, were on the market for $50 in the 1930s.

Cooper was elected member for Esquimalt in the second Vancouver Island legislative assembly in 1860, along with Dr. Helmcken. Cooper resigned in October and moved to New Westminster.[11] He was back in Victoria a few years later, in the hotel business so presumably in the liquor trade again, as reported in the Colonist in 1869: "**The Beehive Hotel** - This old and

---

9 The Robert Melrose diary notes the two-day auction at which Captain Cooper's household effects were sold, perhaps to help finance the journey? The Coopers were back in the colony by 1860.

10 Letter to the Duke of Newcastle, May 4, 1860. Vancouver Island, Governor Douglas, Correspondence Outward, 1859-1864.

11 How satisfiying for Harbour Master Cooper when he went aboard HMS Forward in 1864 to greet Frederick Seymour, successor to his old foe Douglas as governor of the mainland colony.

well-known establishment has passed from Mr. Thomas' hands into those of Capt. James Cooper, late harbour master, who has resigned his situation under the government and accepted 18 months pay in lieu of continuing in office."

The last known record of Captain Cooper in Victoria is in T. N. Hibben's 1877 directory where he is listed as "Agent, Marine and Fisheries, res. Gonzalo House, Victoria District." He is said to have taken his family to California, possibly returning to England later.

Carolyn Fellowes with her husband's brother and sister-in-law, Mr. and Mrs. Alfred Fellowes, their children and a nurse, were early tenants at Cooper's waterfront cottage, ca. 1860. Mrs. Fellowes was the daughter of Sir Rowland Hill, British postal reformer and inventor of the penny postage stamp. (BCARS 5526)

The Two Faces Of Craigflower

The 750-acre property east of Cooper's place was reserved by Chief Factor Douglas before any land was sold to independent settlers. It was earmarked for the Puget's Sound Agricultural Company (PSAC) which was created by the Hudson's Bay Company in 1839 to direct agricultural activities in the Oregon and Washington territories. The Company lost the huge Fort Vancouver and Nisqually farms to the United States after the 49th parallel boundary was set in 1846, but PSAC directors in London were convinced that similarly profitable farms could be established on Vancouver Island. They continued to keep the faith for over a decade, ignoring local reports to the contrary.

Craigflower and three other PSAC farms were to supply meat and vegetables, dairy products, lumber and ironmongery for the new colony/HBC establishment, and bread, biscuits and fresh food for the Royal Navy and other customers.

Governor/Chief Factor Douglas, reluctantly accepting the inevitability of settlers, would have liked a disciplined rural Utopia managed by bailiffs (farm managers) from the gentry with happy labourers and their families recruited in the Old Country. But he was well aware of the difficulties the newcomers would face. He wrote in 1848:

"The first settlers in this country will have many difficulties to contend with, first the scarcity and

quality of food, the want of society - exposure to the weather, - and generally speaking, the absence of every thing like comfort: secondly, the annoyance of the Indians and the petty depredations to which the best of them would be tempted by the careless habits of awkward settlers."

He urged the company directors to offer land as encouragement:

"Amid such discouraging circumstances they would become discontented unless they had some powerful motive to attach them to the country. I would therefore recommend that a free grant of 2 or 300 acres of land be ... made to each family, to give them property interest in the country."

London didn't listen. Advertisements offering land on the remote island colony for $5 an uncleared acre were, understandably, unsuccessful in recruiting colonists as required under the terms of the lease of Vancouver Island.

The directors went ahead with plans for company-financed farms with Douglas as local agent. Two bailiffs were recruited in England and one, Kenneth McKenzie, in Scotland. There is hardly any information about how the bailiffs were selected or why they chose to leave England. Did they find the HBC propaganda irresistible or were there financial difficulties that made the move expedient?[12]

---

12 McKenzie's possible motive for moving from the farm he managed in East Lothian is mentioned in *Canada's Heritage in Scotland* by Ged Martin and Jeffery Simpson (Dundurn Press, Toronto and Oxford, 1989): "In this gentle countryside, it is hard to think of a farmer who failed to make ends meet, but back in the 1840s, Kenneth McKenzie got into serious financial trouble running the Renton estate. In 1851 he sold up and got a job leading a party of emigrants to the new and remote colony of Vancouver Island. In his new home, he

Each was responsible for bringing out labouring families to work the farms. All immigrants brought out under this scheme, although employees of the Hudson's Bay Company, could reasonably be passed off as genuine colonists to satisfy the home government. Douglas had to accept the decision and deal with the aggravation that followed until the PSAC gave up after 15 unprofitable years.

Kenneth McKenzie of Haddingtonshire, Scotland, signed on in 1852 as bailiff for the farm called Craigflower, after the country estate of HBC Governor Andrew Colville. He, his wife Agnes and their five children, Mrs. McKenzie's brother Thomas and sister Isabella, and men hired as carpenters, blacksmiths and labourers and their families set sail on the *Norman Morison* in August, 1852. Besides personal belongings, the ship carried machinery for a steam sawmill and farm implements bought by McKenzie at Company expense.

They arrived at Victoria six months later and expected some sort of welcome on their arrival at the fort on a dismal January day. But like others before him McKenzie was misled by the Company's exaggerated claims about life in the distant colony. He thought he would find a suitable house on a large country estate ready on arrival. Instead, his family and workers were herded into a barracks-like building within Fort Victoria. Like ex-governor Blanshard, Chaplain Robert Staines, Captain Edward Langford of the Colwood Farm and all emigrants since 1849, he felt he was being shabbily treated by the autocratic Company officers.

McKenzie's daughter Wilhelmina Ann, known as Goodie because she was such a remarkably well-be-

Kenneth McKenzie, Craigflower Farm bailiff. (BCARS 3357)

haved baby on the voyage, recounted the family story of their arrival.[13]

"A cold winter day and no one to meet us and we were so eager to be welcomed. It was as if everyone had hidden away from us, ashamed of what they had to offer. By and by along came Mr. Macdonald (afterward Senator), who was then a clerk in the Company's store. He took us to the only place available, a great loft with no partitions, and there we were housed, every one of us, for the time being.

"My father was so angry that he would have taken all of us and gone straight back to Scotland if that had been possible. But when the officials of the company met him they had many excuses and begged him to wait until he saw the place they proposed to have him make his home. A trip up the Gorge water followed, and the site they had chosen was so beautiful that my father's resentment was appeased."

Within a week the appeased and energetic McKenzie had all the single men working on buildings at the site Douglas had chosen for reasons other than its suitability for agriculture. The blacksmith shop and the sawmill, run by a small steam engine brought out from England, were built first. Houses for the workers and their families followed.

There are two versions of life at Craigflower Farm: the idyllic life of a happy and prosperous estate as recalled by Miss McKenzie, and the harsher side described in surviving letters, diaries and official correspondence. First, the McKenzie family life in early colonial days.

---

built a replica of Renton Hall and called it Craigflower. In due course he lost that too, but Craigflower remains one of the gems of Victoria."

13 This and all following quotes of the late Miss McKenzie are from *Pioneer Women of Vancouver Island*, by N. de B. Lugrin, with kind permission from the Women's Canadian Club of Victoria. Miss McKenzie was interviewed in the early 1920s at Lakehill Farm where she had lived since the family moved from Craigflower in 1865.

Miss McKenzie Remembers

Although she was too young to remember the arrival herself, Goodie must have heard the story many times. Her memory for details was said to be excellent when she was interviewed in the mid-1920s by N. de B. Lugrin.

"At first our cooking was all done out of doors. We had to make our own bricks for the fireplaces and chimneys. I remember how delighted father was when he discovered the deposit of limestone. He was walking along a trail and stumbled against a rock. It proved to be limestone. We had a quarry there at once, and building was much simplified.

"Large brick ovens were constructed, and HMS Trincomalee then in port, sent over their bakers to make big batches of bread and cake for the navy. The ships were always supplied from our ovens with what, in those days, they used to call soft bread as distinguished from the ship's biscuits, or hard tack.

"Before the horses came from Nisqually we had oxen to do the ploughing and hauling. In fact we liked the oxen best. The horses were apt to be fractious, but the oxen were always steady and dependable.

"We were happy as children to run wild after restricted nursery life in Scotland. Mother found it difficult. She had brought two servants, but there was such a lack of white women that they married, almost at once ... she was obliged to have Indian help. At first we were afraid, we little girls and mother. We had heard terrible stories before we left home. The Indians of Esquimalt and even the Songhees were very curious about us, especially us little girls with our long, light, fluffy hair. They would come from miles around to watch us at play.

"Each morning we had drill, summoned by the bell. The bugle was blown for roll call and military drill, and each night our one small cannon was fired and every man set off his musket, while mother fired her horse pistol. Even after we knew there was not the slightest danger from the natives, we still kept up the

Miss Goodie McKenzie as a young lady, ca. 1868. (BCARS 3845)

After a short stay in a small house near the fort the McKenzie family lived in this modest cabin similar to those of the 'labouring servants' until the large house was finished in 1855. The Robert Melrose diary notes that "Mr. McKenzie and wife & family removed to the farm" on April 1. (BCARS 58223)

practice, which was always a source of interest and excitement to us children and the Indians.

"We children could talk chinook fluently, all of our servants being Indians. The chief at Esquimalt, Sisiwaka, had two daughters, but not the same wife. He had any number of wives and children. His daughters Lucy and Polly, were very jealous of one another. Both worked for us and each thought her mother the superior wife. They had a lot of dignity and we must treat them with every respect. Polly would draw herself very erect when mother reproved her. 'Remember I am a chief's daughter,' she reminded us. There was a parrot from the navy who used to say pretty Polly, and the real Polly nearly fainted from amazement and fright, then boasted to Lucy."

Goodie remembered a potlach given by Chief Sisiwaka. "It seemed to me there were thousands of Indians there. But it was long ago, nearly seventy years. I cannot remember very well. I know that Lucy stood on the flat roof of her father's lodge and called out the names of those who were to receive the gifts. The Indians would advance in a very surly manner and accept what was offered without a word of thanks. Of course when one remembers that all presents had to be returned in something of at least like value, perhaps this not surprising."

Riding parties were a favorite amusement. "Sometimes we went to the fort by trail, and sometimes we made the journey by boat. Then if the tide was running high at the Gorge, we must wait till the water was quiet unless there was another boat waiting below or above the falls."

The Gorge was also used for traffic between the fort and the naval station when the seas were rough. Boats came up the Arm, as it was called, and portaged to Esquimalt Harbour across Craigflower property.

The most famous visitor who came up the Gorge was not mentioned in Miss McKenzie's reminiscences. In 1861 Lady Jane Franklin, widow of the Arctic explorer, was in Victoria during a round-the-world voyage with her niece, Sophia Cracroft. On March 21 they were whisked from the fort by canoes paddled by Canadians for a 'pic-nic' at Craigflower. Miss Cracroft[14] wrote about it, and the Colonist reported it the next day. Neither account mentioned the Craigflower bailiff or his wife. Miss Cracroft describes "the H. B. Cos farm at Craigflower with its hamlet, biscuit

One of the buildings in this photo is said to be the 'biscuit factory.' An 1850s letter from a naval officer testifies to the quality of the Craigflower biscuits which travelled well, having neither weevils nor mould even when the ship reached Valparaiso. (BCARS 8509)

---

14 *Lady Franklin visits the Pacific Northwest:* Extracts from Letters, edited by Dorothy Blakey Smith, Provincial Archives of British Columbia, Memoir No. XI. pp 76-77.

A stroll along Craigflower bridge in the early 1860s. (BCARS 93608)

manufactory and school" where they landed for luncheon, "several other persons having arrived in boats from Victoria."

The Colonist account notes that a portage was made at the riffles (or falls) and the party "soon after reached Craigflower, where a collation was spread, and everything passed off pleasantly and agreeably." The party spent two hours at Craigflower before the boats moved off and "a parting salute was fired by parties on the shore."

Picnics were a popular pastime. An invitation from Lettie Tuzo, wife of Dr. Henry Atkinson Tuzo, inviting the McKenzies to join them for a picnic in their garden at Parson's Bridge, is preserved with the McKenzie papers at the B.C. archives.

Social life was enlivened by visits from naval officers and invitations to visit the ships. Goodie remembers going to a ball when she was much too young, but the shortage of females in those years was so acute her mother reluctantly allowed her to go with her older sisters.

Goodie McKenzie was 15 years old when the family moved to Lakehill in 1866.

Cousin Alice Also Remembers

Another little girl, Goodie's cousin Alice Russell, also grew up at Craigflower. Her parents were Thomas Russell, Mrs. McKenzie's brother, and his wife, Sarah Collier, who came from England in 1857 and stayed with the McKenzies for two years before her marriage.

"She met my father there at mealtimes, as he slept at the Office, always busy helping Mr. McKenzie. An Indian was courier for letters to Miss Collier when she was alone. He would tap his shirt pocket, and she would find an opportunity to receive it.

"The roar of tumbling waters from the Gorge at low tide made a lullaby for me," Alice recalled. Her father was schoolmaster at Craigflower for a short time, but his principal role was as commissariat or dispenser of provisions for families. "Of course at times there was much grumbling but my father told them that he could give them only what he was authorized to give." The little girl heard stories of tea parties, when the women "indulging in afternoon tea with their friends found their tea supply running short and hoped by threats to get more but found that is was not obtained so easily. Long afterwards my father remarked to me 'Perhaps they never saw tea in the old country.'"

She describes the farm "when things were in running order ... a store, a kiln to dry wheat and oats, and mills for flour and oatmeal, also baker's ovens, and a place to kill and dress beef and other meats."[15]

Years later she watched as her parents' little log house was rafted across the Arm and rebuilt under the maple tree at the schoolhouse. Alice Russell Michaels and her sister, whose portraits hang in the restored schoolhouse, grew up to be a teachers themselves.

The Other Side of the Story

'The Puget Sound Company bought all these lands and spent a heap of money in developing them, but proved a failure.' J. S. Helmcken, Reminiscences.

All was not well at the farm. Kenneth McKenzie was not a generous employer. Within a few weeks of their arrival at Craigflower some of his men were refusing to work and one of his land stewards deserted.

An entry in McKenzie's journal for April 21, 1853, lists absentees: "Robert Anderson, Andrew Hume, George Deans, Duncan Lidgate, James Downie and Mr. Weir - absent with complaints to Mr. Douglas about food."

A later entry suggests the complaints were not unfounded: "Old cow received from [Chief Factor John] Work and [given] out as follows: Anderson, 20 pounds beef, Lidgate 14, Hume 11, Deans 10 ..." and the other workmen's families, while superior meat from a young bullock was "reserved for young men and my own family."

Workers were still punished with imprisonment for disobedience or insubordination. In May George Deans, a carpenter, "refused order for work, and very insolent at same time struck work." Annie Deans wrote home to Scotland about her Geordie's time "in the chokie." Other absentees included the blacksmith, but land steward James Stewart seems to have been one of the few employees McKenzie could rely on. Geordie and others left to work for Cooper for a time, then at the fort. They found this, Annie says in a one of her letters, far more agreeable.

McKenzie's most violent reaction to insubordination is mentioned in an intriguing one-liner in Robert Melrose's diary: "Mr. McKenzie shot up Bartleman's cas-

Thomas Russell, McKenzie's brother-in-law, and family, possibly on the grounds of Craigflower School where Russell was a reluctant schoomaster in 1865. He complained a lot about too little pay for "my various duties in the Bakery, Butchery the mills & C." (BCARS 3987)

---

15 Alice Michael's reminiscences in B.C. Heritage Properties files.

Craigflower Boundaries

In 1858 A. G. Dallas provided a full description of Craigflower Farm. It consisted of 752.5 acres, less 170.5 allotted to retired servants, leaving 582 acres. 80 of these were in cultivation, 70 were open pasture and 432 were barren rock or heavy timber. "The Farm is bounded as follows: On the South and South East by Constance Cove Farm from which it is separated by a Log Fence, -- from South to West by Equimalt Harbour, -- the Indian Reservation aforementioned, and the farm known as Captain Cooper's - from which it is separated by a Log fence, -- and from the South East to North, and thence to West, by a winding arm of the Sea, which runs up from Victoria Harbour. On the other side of this Arm there are 36 acres (included in the above quantity) still belonging to the Farm - being the remainder of its land in the Section after deducting the allotments made to Servants. These 36 acres (consisting of Rock and Wood) run along the Banks of the said Arm in a North Easterly direction: On the East, they are bounded by the Land attached to Maple Point School and the allotment to Servants... All the land in cultivation is fenced, partly with Logs, and partly with Posts and Rails of Split and Sawn Timber; The greatest portion of the remainder, on the sides not bounded by water, is fenced with Logs."

tle." The 'castle' was Peter Bartleman's blacksmith shop on Craigflower property where he did work for other customers in his spare time. After a dispute over Bartleman's use of scarce coal for non-company work, McKenzie exploded and destroyed the moonlighting blacksmith's premises. McKenzie demanded that Bartleman be deported back to England. Douglas refused - skilled labour was hard to find - and Bartleman was then free to set up shop on Cooper's land up the hill from Craigflower.

At its most productive the farm carved out of the forest had carpenter's shops, blacksmith shops, a steam sawmill, flour mill, brick kiln and slaughterhouse, and was a major part of the life of the colony for 13 years. But it never made money for the company.

Correspondence to and from company directors in London and official records are filled with accounts of mismanagement, labour trouble and complaints from headquarters about lack of profits plaguing the four PSAC farms.

Back in 1848 Douglas warned the Company directors in London that "a newly opened farm in this country makes no return the first year, the second year it supplies the labourer with food, and the third year it will yield enough for food and clothing, provided there be a market for grain. It is therefore important that a settler should have means enough to support himself for a couple of years, or he will involve himself hopelessly in debt, and never thrive."

Early panoramic view of Craigflower Farm showing the school at right, McKenzie's house on the rise behind the bridge, barns across the road and bake house, mills and smithy at left, on the site of the present Craigflower Motel. (BCARS 24492)

Since the PSAC was footing the bills, under the terms of contracts with the bailiffs, the debts of thousands of pounds were laid at its door. Charge accounts at the Company store added considerably to the debt. As historian Derek Pethick said of the lavishly hospitable bailiff of Colwood Farm, Captain Langford "was per-

haps the first British Columbian to grasp the possibilities of the expense account."[16] McKenzie had a fair grasp of the system too, but his extravagances tended to be more in the nature of new machinery and equipment ordered from Britain without permission.

Flaws in the Grand Scheme

The concept that worked well for the magnificent establishment at Fort Vancouver, and even the smaller Fort Nisqually which produced fine sheep and horses, was never successfully adapted to the rocks and swamps of the Esquimalt farms. Basic flaws included:

Unsuitable Land

Douglas chose land for Craigflower and Captain Langford's Mill Farm that was not suited for the type of agriculture envisioned in London. The sites looked attractive, but rocky, heavily forested Vancouver Island did not have the agricultural potential of the 4,000-acre Fort Vancouver establishment, Douglas's former post. Most of the best land was already in the HBC reserve east of the fort, so the newcomers were left with some astonishingly inappropriate acreage to the west.

Despite reports from more knowledgeable people on the spot, including colonial surveyor J. D. Pemberton, the London directors refused to believe there were difficulties of clearing land and making it productive. Sublimely ignorant of local conditions, they continued to issue orders impossible to carry out. As an

example: The price of flour went sky-high during the California gold rush, so they insisted that wheat for flour should be the main crop. By the time their orders reached the colony the temporarily inflated price had dropped drastically. Yet their out-dated orders had to be carried out.

Erratic Management

Management, both London and local, left much to be desired. The PSAC choice of farm bailiffs seems remarkably haphazard. The directors, all members of the board of the Hudson's Bay Company, had other prob-

Formal portraits of the McKenzies show the girls and their mother dressed in gowns made from the same pattern with yokes and flounces slightly modified for individuality. Standing, left to right, are Dorothea, Jessie and Wilhelmina Ann, known as Goodie. Agnes (Russell) McKenzie is seated next to eldest daughter Agnes. The clothes suggest the picture was taken sometime around 1868. (BCARS 3365)

---

16 PETHICK, Derek: Victoria: The Fort. Vancouver, Mitchell Press Limited, 1968. Highly recommended for further reading about Colonial Victoria.

lems and were inclined to dismiss letters from Vancouver Island as snivelling complaints. They remained convinced that the farms could be as profitable as any in the Empire.

Locally, McKenzie could have used a course in man-management. He knew his sheep, but was not tactful in supervising independent-minded Scots who didn't like being treated as serfs. Alexander Grant Dallas, head of the HBC Western Department and yet another son-in-law of Douglas, reported that McKenzie's management "has been a total failure" and that although he was "well-meaning and thoroughly honest" he had a hasty temper and unsound judgement, and "... a more unfit man ... could not have been selected to exercise the control and direction of affairs ... "[17]

Errors in Judgement:

Men sent out as carpenters were expected to carry out any task, however menial (as mutineering miners had been three years earlier). HBC officers made no distinction between skilled tradesmen and mere labourers of 'the lower orders.' They continued to expect unquestioning obedience, an old-fashioned management policy that had worked in fur-trade days.

Douglas's suggestion that colonists be granted their own land would probably have worked better. Most of the men who completed their five-year contracts took up their 20-acre grants and bought more land as they could afford it.

McKenzie, considered the most competent of the gentleman farmers, was made general supervisor of the other company farms and, along with the equally unqualified Langford and the third bailiff, Thomas Skinner of Constance Cove Farm, was appointed a justice of the peace in 1854. They were inexperienced, and unsuccessful, in this role as well.

The McKenzie family moved to a large sheep farm at Lakehill (which included Christmas Hill and extended south of the present McKenzie Avenue) in 1866. He died in 1874 at the age of 63. Mrs. McKenzie lived until 1897.

Kenneth McKenzie, seated left, and son Kenneth right. Standing, left to right, are Andrew Colville McKenzie (named after the Hudson's Bay Company governor of the time; Robert Gregory McKenzie and William Blair McMenzie.(BCARS 3361)

---

17 Letter to H.B.C. Governor H. H. Berens, cited in *The Puget's Sound Agricultural Company on Vancouver Island*, Brian C. Coyle, MA thesis, Simon Fraser University, 1977. p.77.

Some Roaring Good Times

The meticulously hand-printed diary was published by R. Melrose, Front Street, Maple Point. Invaluable as a day-to-day account of life at Craigflower, it has been used by scores of researchers. The Haddington men had the benefit of a Scots education, but they also had a thirst for a dram or two. December 25, 1855, there was a "Christmas Ball celebrated with great glee." Melrose notes the day the schoolhouse was raised and "whole company notoriously drunk." Lesser celebrations see people like James Stewart only "¼ drunk, the author whole drunk." On the serious side, he reports on meetings of the Scientific Institute, held regularly at the schoolhouse on subjects such as The Pleasures of Studying the Sciences, the Discoveries of Optical Sciences (given by the author) and The Nobility of Man by shepherd James Deans - all swotted up from books brought out from Scotland. Melrose and the workmen were aware of the world outside the farm. He notes a public meeting in February, 1854, on "the state of the Colony" at which a subscription "set agoing in purpose to send Mr. Staines home to lay the proceedings before the house of Parliament. God Speed." Births, deaths, celebrations, shortages of liquor are all noted, much to the delight of today's readers. Thank you, Robert Melrose.

Next to Helmcken, Robert Melrose is a researcher's best friend, for his account of "Five Years Servitude Under the Hudson's Bay Company on Vancouver Island." Despite the title the author and his fellow workmen had some roaring good times, rated by the author according to the degree of intoxication achieved by the lads. (BCARS 3594)

Derelict Melrose house, one of the last surviving Craigflower cottages, photographed ca. 1931. (BCARS 18393)

Voting Day at Craigflower

Craigflower farmhouse was a polling place for the 1863 election of members of the Vancouver Island House of Assembly. A copy of the public notices dated July 16, 1863, is preserved in the McKenzie papers:

"I Kenneth McKenzie, returning officer for the district of Esquimalt & Metchosin do hereby give Public Notice that I shall proceed to the election of two members to serve in parliament for the said districts on Tuesday the 21st day of July at 11 o'clock in the forenoon at Craigflower Farm in the District of Esquimalt, at which time and place all persons entitled

The parlour of the restored farmhouse, much as it would have looked when Dr. Helmcken celebrated his election victory there in 1860. The furniture includes some original McKenzie pieces and a horsehair sofa from the Stewart family. (Robert Duffus photo)

to vote at the said election are requested to give their attendance."

Among those entitled to vote were several Victoria luminaries who owned land near Craigflower, Deadman's River or Parson's Bridge. The list includes attorney general George Hunter Cary, who owned two waterfront lots behind the Four Mile House; Thomas Flewin and George Foster, Deadman's River; Thomas Harris, first mayor of Victoria, land adjoining Deadman's River; John McGregor with 181 acres on Rowe's Stream; William Richard Parson, Arthur Peatt, Henry Piers and James Porter, all owning land "nr. Bridge on Rowe's Stream"; Caleb Pike who was living at the Four Mile House and owned house and land on Cooper's Section 3 near Craigflower; James Stewart, "on the farm on the main road, rental of land over 20 pounds per annum"; Henry Atkinson Tuzo, a doctor, living near Parson's Bridge, Kenneth McKenzie, "rental over 12 pounds per annum," and the successful candidates, John Sebastian Helmcken and Robert Burnaby.

Victory Party

This was Helmcken's third successful election. He wrote about a victory party at Craigflower after the 1860 election when the other successful candidate was James Cooper: Mrs. McKenzie "gave a jolly good dinner, i.e. self and Burnaby and friends. The men regaled themselves in the kitchen and after a while came in to congratulate us - Burnaby sang some comic songs - in fact there was a feast of reason and a flow of soul till midnight. The McKenzies were whole-souled people and felt the victory as much or more than the candidates, for not much love existed between them and the Langfords, Skinners and Coopers, but they were not enemies. Cooper resigned afterwards and Burnaby was elected."

The Naval Connection

The head of Esquimalt Harbour provided two things essential for Royal Navy ships — fresh water and a safe place for a powder magazine.

The first hydrographic survey of Esquimalt Harbour was begun in 1846. Lieutenant James Wood of the brig Pandora was in charge of the survey with naval instructor Robert Mills Inskip and his junior officers from HMS Fisgard assisting. View Royal bays, coves and islands named during this survey include Dyke Point, after Second Lieutenant Charles Dyke, and Paterson Point after Third Lieutenant George Yates Paterson. HMS Fisgard was on station from 1843 to 1847.

While the Hudson's Bay Company was establishing its predominance on the land, the British Admiralty was beginning to think seriously about Esquimalt Harbour as a useful Pacific base. The Crimean War, and

Ships also filled their water barrels from a stream flowing into Limekiln Cove. It ran from a spring higher up Helmcken Road and was said to have provided a steady supply of ice-cold water year-round. The site is marked by a cairn erected by the Thermopylae Club in 1959. (Michael Pope photos)

associated skirmishes in Alaska, made the proposition even more pressing.

Ships anchoring near the present Dockyard found the lack of fresh water on the Esquimalt side a nuisance. An officer of one of the ships, probably HMS Dido, wrote in 1854:

"There is a stream of water at the extreme N. [of the harbour] called Rowe's stream, where we watered, sending our pinnace up and filling her in bulk from the mill stream by hoses, which was often tedious work as the water ran very slowly. The flour mill belonging to the company stands on the left hand going up stream and abreast of it [is] a sawmill. These will soon be superseded, as at Craigflower steam is already in use for a sawmill and no doubt will shortly be used for a flour mill."[18]

Contemporary photos show where the flume was built between two falls. Iron rings at the top of the rock were thought to have anchored part of the HBC mill dam until recently-discovered historic photos show the location of the flumes. (Maureen Duffus photos)

Impatient with filling barrels with fresh water at Mill-stream one by one, the Royal Navy constructed a flume graded from the 20-foot high ledge of the falls to sea level at a point near the west side of Parson's Bridge. The photos are believed to have been taken in the 1870s. Parts of the structure remained as late as the 1920s, as recalled by residents of neighbouring properties. (National Archives of Canada, prints cour-

---

18 Typescript, Pollock collection, no source given.

Magazine Island

The little island is only 400 feet long and 200 feet wide. It was named after Edmund Picoti Cole, master of HMS Fisgard during Admiralty surveys in 1846, and served as a naval ammunition depot from 1859 to 1938. Building began six years before the naval station at Esquimalt was officially established in 1865. Orders for construction of the first two powder magazines were given by Colonel Richard Clement Moody of the Royal Engineers and Admiral Sir Robert Baynes, RN, in 1859. The original 30' by 50' guardhouse, built of brick and wood, was completed later that year.[19]

On March 8, 1862, Captain A. M. Parsons of the Royal Engineers, stationed at New Westminster, inserted a notice in the British Colonist:

"Tenders are invited by the Colonel commanding the troops for chopping, burning off and thoroughly cleaning all the trees, underbrush and etc., on Cole Island, at the head of Esquimalt Harbour ..." Trees were to be cut "at chopping height" and underbrush cut to the ground. No trees or brush would be allowed to fall into the water, and the shoreline of the island "is to be carefully cleared of all timber and logs to low water mark." Tenders were to be sent to New Westminster, the work to be completed within 14 days of acceptance. The Royal Navy was anxious to get on with building its ammunition depot on the rocky island a safe distance away from the anchorage across the harbour.

By 1862 the Admiralty thought it prudent to secure ownership of the rocky islet. The Hudson's Bay Company was requested to place Cole Island at Colonel Moody's disposal, "to preserve the island from sale or pre-emption." Polite letters passed between the colonial secretary, the surveyor general for the colony and Colonel Moody. "I have the honor," wrote the colonial surveyor, "to report to you, that I have received His Excellency's instructions ... to hand over the Island to you officially, which order you will be pleased to con-sider carried into effect from and after the 10th of March, 1862."[20]

At the height of its importance, from the first visit of the magnificent Flying Squadron in 1871 until the departure of the British fleet in 1905, it had as many as 16 solidly constructed buildings connected by wooden walkways for safe storage and transport of powder and ammunition.

The island served as the Royal Navy's ammunition depot until 1905 and was transferred to the Canadian Navy on November 9, 1910, as part of the Esquimalt

Zinc-clad shed in this 1977 photo is thought to have been one of the original powder magazines. It was approximately the size of a building described in a British Admiralty statement of 1912 which listed an 1859 powder magazine, zinc on wood, 35' by 18'. To house the volatile black powder of the time, timber frames were clad with wood sheathing covered with zinc. (Parks Canada photo)

---

19 Memorandum, naval historian E. C. Russell, Ottawa, July 1958, to Deputy Minister, Department of Northern Affairs and National Resources. Copy, Naval Museum, H.M.C.S. Naden.

20 Letters cited in Willard Ireland's paper *Title to and Description of the Properties comprising the Esquimalt Naval Base*, B.C.A.R.S. 1942. He states that no further records of transfer of title have been found, due to confusion resulting when Vancouver Island was returned to the Crown after the Hudson's Bay Company's stewardship ended.

The first powder magazines looked like unimpressive little tin sheds beside their grander brick and masonry neighbours, including the remaining two-storey shell storage buildings which dominate the north side of the island. Most were built between 1875 and 1898. (Maureen Duffus photo)

naval establishment. The Colonist reported the transfer:

"At noon today a Union Jack will be hauled down from the flag staff at Esquimalt naval yards and another one hoisted. It will mark the transfer to the Canadian Naval Department by the British Admiralty."

Choice of the island for the powder magazines seems to have been made originally on its safe distance from the main naval activity across the harbour at Esquimalt. It was not the most convenient site. Only small boats and flat-bottom barges could be used for transporting ammunition and supplies. At low tide it is surrounded by mud flats. Fresh water had to be brought from dockyard, or, at one time, through an underwater pipeline from the View Royal shore.

Cole Island was virtually abandoned during the 1930s after years of pressure from local military personnel to move the depot to a larger, safer location. Large con-

crete magazines on the south shore of the harbour were completed in 1938, but a few of the old buildings were used for ships' stores and some army field artillery as late as 1944.

Little Orphan Island

Cole Island has lost most of its unique heritage buildings, the only examples of their kind in western Canada. Lack of interest in Ottawa and bureaucratic buck-passing from provincial to federal and back to provincial governments have combined to allow destruction or dismantling of most of the buildings.

It could have been worse. The old directive to "preserve the island from sale or pre-emption" was forgotten in 1958 when the island was declared surplus and handed over to Crown Assets for disposal.

This misguided attempt to sell part of the country's naval heritage did not sit well, even in Ottawa. A memorandum from naval historian E. C. Russell recommended that the federal Department of Northern Affairs and Natural Resources consider Cole Island a national historic site.

"It is doubtful if any of the [surviving] buildings in the dockyard proper go back as far as some of the buildings of Cole Island ... It will be noted that the Cole Island buildings date from as early as 1859 and all of these pre-date the formal establishment of Esquimalt Naval Base ... by Imperial Order in Council dated 29 June 1865."[21]

The island was taken off the market. But not before several View Royal residents put in bids ranging from $1 to $5,000, all promising loving care and attention. Other hopeful purchasers just wanted to knock down the buildings and sell the old bricks.

Then the Historic Sites and Monuments Board came into the picture. Jack Rippengale, superintendent of Fort Rodd Hill in 1962, explained how the bungling came about: The army establishment and Fisgard lighthouse were declared national historic sites, but as Cole Island was a naval establishment and not histori-

---

21 RUSSELL, E.C., *Disposal of Magazine Buildings Cole Island, Esquimalt*, Memorandum to Deputy Minister Hamilton, Department of Northern Affairs and National Resources, Ottawa, July 11, 1958: copy, Naval Museum, H.M.C.S. Naden.

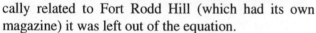

cally related to Fort Rodd Hill (which had its own magazine) it was left out of the equation.

"The question should have been whether or not the Island and its buildings were of historic significance in their own right. Parks Canada, by then the caretaker of Fort Rodd Hill, didn't consider this, so the Island became a poor relative, and that's a shame." Several buildings were considered unsafe so Parks Canada, fearful of lawsuits in case of accidents, took them down instead of repairing them. A team of architects spent several months making detailed records and drawings of the buildings as they were then, so some sort of reconstruction is still possible. Rippengale says 20,000 bricks from the dismantled buildings were carefully cleaned of mortar and stored for this purpose.

Lloyd Brooks, former deputy minister of B.C's Parks and Recreation ministry, adds: "The excuse given that Fort Rodd Hill was basically an armoury, and that the naval magazine was incompatible with the Army establishment, was feeble. The finger points at members

Ruins of the oldest and largest mine and shell storage building, above, stood dangerously at the northwest corner of the island until dismantled brick by brick. Remains of the wooden walkways connecting buildings and loading docks, top, have also been removed. The gaping hole in building at top left shows how vandals prised away bricks leaving a room with a view. The remaining buildings have been closed off by massive steel doors to prevent further vandalism. (Parks Canada photos)

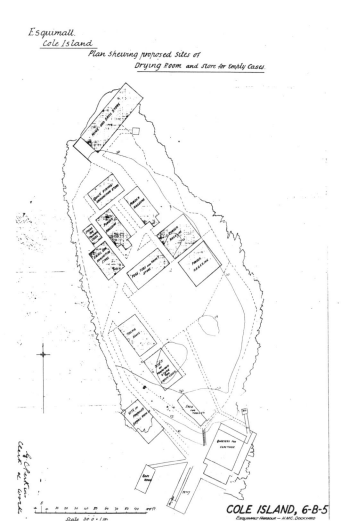

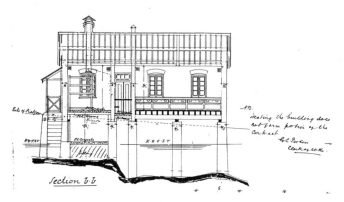

Clerk of Works G. S. Perkins signed these undated plans, above, for proposed storage and drying rooms. His site plan (ca. 1890), shows the drying room would have been southwest of the jetty using walls from an old building. There is no evidence that it was ever built. (Original drawings filed with B.C. Heritage Properties)

of the Historic Sites and Monuments Board, all but one Easterners, who called the shots. They decreed that the buildings, a mere 100 years old, did not warrant historic preservation. And there was a weasel clause in the papers transferring the Island to Parks Canada to the effect that if the island was considered surplus to requirements it would be handed back to the Province. And so Cole Island fell through the cracks."

By the time it came under the protection of British Columbia Heritage Properties as an undeveloped historic site, much was lost. With regrettable disregard for the

island's unique naval heritage, looters, vandals and thieves had already destroyed many of the buildings. Bricks were pried out until walls collapsed. One roof was found sitting on the floor of a vanished building, while another sagged dangerously on wobbly makeshift props. In another half a dozen 12-inch-thick planks were sawn off by an ambitious looter, leaving the ends on both sides attached to the hefty roof beams. One building was nearly blown up by a teenage vandal.

The cheekiest thief of all managed to move a massive 14-inch square timber across a building, but couldn't get it out the door. He tacked a note on it saying "Please Don't Take."

For now, only the locals in canoes, rowboats or kayaks enjoy the unusual little islet still known as Magazine Island. A family of otters used to inhabit the rocks or the landing dock, but they have decamped - the dock is falling apart - leaving it to the playful seals who surface to investigate visiting boaters. Trees and brush have grown up again, old lilac bushes struggle to survive on the rocks, and the periwinkle planted around the caretaker's garden provides groundcover on the century-old building sites.

The delightful little island, rimmed with arbutus trees leaning out over the water, has been a favorite spot for almost everyone who grew up around the View Royal waterfront. It used to be a wonderful place for boating expeditions, especially at dusk when the echoes in the old arched loading bays were deliciously ghostly.

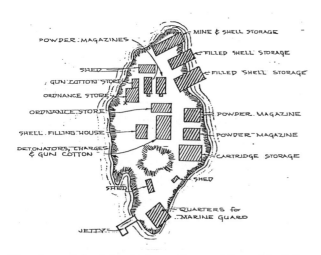

Site plan of the island shows the position of buildings approximately as the young bugler Redvers Smith would have known them in 1915. (R. L. Clapp drawing for Parks Canada, 1972)

Bugler on Guard Duty

(From an interview taped by Shoreline School students)

During World War I the guardhouse on Cole Island was occupied by naval personnel on seven-day tours of duty. One of these was the late Redvers Smith, who joined the navy as a bugler in 1915 at the age of 15. In an interview taped by Shoreline School students in 1985 he recalled:

"A security party was sent to the island where they remained for one week. The party was changed every week, and consisted of a leading seaman or petty officer in charge, and about five seamen, of which two would be on watch at one time, one in the building where ammunition was stored and the other down on the landing float on the other side of the island. The fifth seaman was a spare and also did the cooking. As I remember the meals were brought over from the barracks cookhouse and sent up, our man just warmed things up.

" On the southeastern corner was the landing float, and [above it] a two-storey building of which the upper floor was used by the naval guard, and the lower floor was occupied by a permanent representative ... of the Dominion police and his wife."

Mr. Smith remembered that among the ammunition stored on the island that wartime May was a barge load from HMS Newcastle, "and I do remember that torpedoes were a part of the equipment."

The island was visited daily by someone from the main dockyard in Esquimalt to check that everything was in order. Seamen in dockyard barracks undergoing training or waiting to be transferred to ships "were not keen on the Cole Island duty, because once you were there you never left it for the full week, but I accepted it as part of the routine and it was a reasonably enjoyable experience. The men slept on hammocks on ship, but the Cole Island quarters were supplied with metal camp beds, so our hammocks became mattress and bedding in the two upstairs rooms where we had our meals and slept."

At low tide "one could almost walk from the land out to the island on the mud. At odd times of night people were out digging clams, perhaps Indians, and then we would be alerted to keep a close eye on them."

Living on Cole Island

Alice (Heron) King

I spent a lot of time on Cole Island in the early 1920s with Aunt Hetta and Uncle Harry Hetherington, who were caretakers for several years. Twice a day the temperature inside the buildings was recorded and a monthly report was sent away. The buildings felt cold and slightly damp - huge heavy doors were kept locked.

As well as the ammunition buildings there were quarters for a guard over the area where my aunt and uncle lived. I only recall a night watchman coming each evening and checking in, and going away again in the morning. Doubtless it was different during the 1914-18 war.

A boat from the dockyard came nearly every day, bringing mail or groceries that had been ordered, and workmen if there was work to be done. A grey rowboat was our local transport and many times my aunt showed me sealife as the tide went out, all so fascinating for a prairie child! The windows in the sitting room were over the water at high tide and one could watch the ducks dive and swim underwater, small crabs crawl over barnacles, and occasional small jellyfish float near shore. Kingfishers also watched from trees not far way. At low tide there were two tiny

An early 1920s snapshot, top, shows the glass-fronted living quarters of the caretaker's family on the side of the 1864 guardhouse, above. A public notice in the Colonist of May 30, 1864, called for tenders for "the erection of a house on Cole Island," specifying "The house to be built on the site of the late guard house, to be built of brick or stone with a slate roof, and to consist of two rooms, with necessary outhouse of brick or wood. The slates for the roofing are already on the spot." (Living quarters photo courtesy Alice King. Guardhouse photo Parks Canada)

beaches. Arbutus leaves and berries and fir needles had to be swept off the board walks and steps.

Aunt Hetta had a few hens, raised a few chickens every year, and also had a small garden for vegetables and flowers on the island. Coal was the fuel for cooking and heating. There was an open grate in the sitting room where we played cribbage and did puzzles, or read out loud, things like Robert Service poems.

Mrs. King found a poem written by a guest of her aunt and uncle at Cole Island:

> *There's a mite of an island named Cole*
> *About seventy leagues south of the pole,*
> *Where they treat you so nice*
> *That you wish to come twice*
> *To this dear little island named Cole.*

It was written by Staff Sgt. H. Daglish, Yukon Infantry, co. C.E.F. (Canadian Expeditionary Force), Dawson, Y.T., on January 1, 1917.

The Mile Houses

Two of the most conspicuous landmarks in View Royal are the Four Mile House and the Six Mile House Hotel. Both began in the 1850s as stopping places between Fort Victoria and the farms to the west, with some stabling for horses and refreshment, including spirits, for thirsty settlers and naval personnel.

G. Durrant. '93

The Calverts' Country Inn

Mary Gouge, daughter of Peter and Elizabeth Calvert, playing for a dance at the Four Mile House, undated. (Wilf Gouge album)

The Four Mile house was built on six acres of land Peter Calvert of Craigflower acquired from James Cooper's Section III. Calvert and his young wife Elizabeth Montgomery, who had been a fellow passenger on the *Norman Morison*, built a house and barn and began farming shortly after Calvert completed his HBC contract in 1858.

The house on the hill west of Craigflower soon became a convenient stopping place for settlers on the way to and from their farms at Metchosin and Sooke. Elizabeth Calvert cooked for the travellers while they rested their horses, and eventually the farmhouse became a small inn, surrounded by gardens and orchards, with an ivy-covered summer house. Mrs. Calvert spoke Chinook and nursed her Indian friends when they were sick. An Indian couple, Joe Snoopin and his wife, did the washing, and another Indian woman known as Shrimpy kept the inn well supplied with shrimp and crabs. Indians came to the house to perform a ritual dance when Elizabeth Calvert died.

When Peter Calvert died his daughter Mary and her husband, Bertrand Gouge, continued to operate the inn. They stayed on in the house and raised their family there. Mary was equally interested in horses and music and played for local dances. Harness racing horses were pastured in nearby fields, and the Four

Four Calvert children were in this Craigflower School class, circa 1887. Fannie and Grace are front row centre, Peter is fifth from the right, centre row, and Joe is standing behind him. (BCARS 14375)

The highway curved dangerously close to the Four Mile House when motor traffic increased. The 1928 photo shows an automobile speeding down the hill some time after another car had knocked the supports out from under the balcony. (BCARS 68646)

Buildings in this undated photo were identified by Wilf Gouge junior as an aviary, dance hall and stables located across the road from the main building. (Wilf Gouge album)

Mile House remained a favourite stopping place on the way to or from Victoria.

One frequent guest was Major J. L. F. MacFarlane whose surveys in the early 1900s led to construction of the road over the Malahat Mountain.[22] His grandson, George MacFarlane, writes:

"Although he lived on his 100-acre farm at Cobble Hill, my grandfather used to travel to Victoria quite often. He always stopped at the Four Mile House the night before he got to Victoria, so that he could get into town early next morning. Then he and his team would head out to the Four Mile the afternoon before the trip back, to avoid the long wait for horses in the crowded livery stables in town."

Prohibition in 1917 put an end to the profitable side of the hotel business. When sale of liquor was again allowed in some places in 1923 Mary's son, Wilf Gouge, tried to have the liquor licence renewed. But the curve of the Four Mile Hill where the house stood was considered too dangerous for imbibing patrons to negotiate in their automobiles.

In its unlicensed days the old house had an interesting assortment of tenants and owners. During the war it was managed by Alex Davidson who ran the restaurant with the help of his son and daughter, Ernest and Kay.

Ernest Davidson at the side door of the Four Mile House when his father Alex managed the restaurant during World War II. (Kay Berry album)

Kay (Davidson) Berry remembers helping with the cleaning and serving when she was only 13 years old. Her brother remembers a large walk-in wine cellar behind the kitchen. After the war the Four Mile House had a short life as a cabaret. An upper room was used for church services for a few months in 1943.

Later the house was a private residence, home of the Galbraith family whose extraordinary collection of miniature shoes and antiques was on display. In 1967, according to a Capital Regional District publication, an American contractor bought it hoping to open a pub and restaurant. Again the liquor licence was denied. After several years of neglect, the empty old building became a halfway house for native parolees, but was so expensive to maintain that the society which ran it had to sell. The house was sold several more times before present owners Graham and Wendy Haymes took possession in 1979.

By then it was woefully dilapidated. Mr. and Mrs. Haymes began careful restoration, living in it while they ran it as a tearoom and furniture showroom. Eventually they acquired the liquor licence denied for 70 years. They now run a restaurant and pub, in greatly enlarged premises, much as the Calverts and Gouges did in earlier days.

---

22 Major MacFarlane carried out his surveys in spite of the general conviction that it would be impossible to build a road through the wooded, mountainous country. With hand compass and aneroid barometer, travelling the E&N tracks on a borrowed hand car, he mapped out a road that includes the route through the Goldstream lowlands and most of the present highway. He was the first to travel the road from Duncan to Victoria on its completion in December, 1911.

The Millwright's Hotel

Former HBC millwright William Richard Parson left the Company sometime in the early 1850s. He had seen other ex-servants make handsome profits in the liquor trade, despite the formidable retail licence fee of £120 a year imposed on liquor vendors in 1853.

Parson first acquired a well-situated piece of property not far from the sawmill. Like the Four Mile House, it was conveniently on the only road to the western farms. The fact that Royal Navy ships came by for water at the millstream was equally attractive. Then in 1856 he paid £75 on account for his first liquor licence. Customers have been stopping at the Six Mile House ever since.

Earliest photographs of the inn show a one-storey verandahed wooden building on a rocky ledge on the eastern side of the rickety bridge - a danger spot as noted in various writings from the time it was built.[23] There was a small stable for horses and refreshment for travellers to Metchosin, Happy Valley and Sooke. Later photographs show the two-storey addition with balcony attached to the original building. Since Parson disappears from archives records after a few years it seems likely he quickly made enough money to retire.

For a few years in the 1870s Peter Calvert of the Four Mile House operated the hotel. But in 1877 the bridge was again declared unsafe and the liquor licence was nearly cancelled. Another proprietor was Cariboo gold rush teamster Henry Price whose nephew succeeded him.

Prohibition from 1917 to 1921 was a setback but there are stories that alcoholic refreshment was available on the premises even then. Nearby Helmcken Bay, a deep, dark cove with few houses in those days, is also said to have had something to do with illegal distribution of liquor to American 'rum-runners' during United States prohibition from 1923 to 1933.

Certainly the hotel prospered when Victoria and Oak Bay chose not to allow the sale of liquor by the glass after 1931. The Six-Mile beer parlour welcomed crowds from the drybelt nightly.

Post-prohibition liquor regulations required a separate entrance for 'Ladies and Escorts' so the front door was moved to the side and two entrances created. Traces of the old verandah can still be seen under the 1940 facing.

The present pub claims to hold the oldest standing liquor licence in British Columbia. Although it was not the first retail licence issued[24] it is certain that none of the other 1850s establishments survive to challenge the claim.

Limekiln Cove seaplane base was on right – some activity during U.S. prohibition.

---

23 See minutes of the House Assembly, 1859, when J.D. Pemberton, MLA and colonial surveyor, objected to alloting funds for improving the bridge on grounds that "all the owners of property thereabouts being wealthy people, could well afford to build a bridge by their subscriptions."

24 The first retail liquor licence went to James Yates, Owner of the Ship Inn on Wharf Street, in March, 1853. The only other licence noted in Hudson's Bay Company accounts that year was held by the Company itself, which paid £100 for a wholesale licence. Total revenue from licence fees the first year was £220.

Progress of the Six Mile House is shown in this series of photographs dating from the early 1860s. The original Six Mile House and the bridge Mr. Parson built in 1855. Canoes on the shore may have brought thirsty sailors from ships across the harbour. (National Archives of Canada, in Esquimalt Municipal Archives collection)

One of the earliest photographs, ca 1865, with British sailor on the bridge. (BCARS 15260)

A decade later, judging by growth of the trees left of the bridge, the outbuildings are enlarged, bridge railings repaired and the dead tree is gone. A Chinese man carries baskets toward the bridge. (BCARS 8059)

The Inn remained much the same until about 1898 when a two-storey structure with a balcony on two sides was added, turning it into the Six Mile House Hotel. The Sooke stage, right, went to Otter Point Road. The man in the front seat holds a horn that was blown to notify homesteaders of a delivery. (BCARS 54985)

A later photo of the present two-storey building was taken before fire destroyed the original building sometime around 1920. The plank bridge appears the same but high centre railings have been added, as in the cover painting. (Esquimalt Archives, Harriet Westby collection)

The 1988 addition built on the site of Mr. Parson's original hotel was photographed in 1993. Foundations of the 1855 building were uncovered as construction for the addition and the garden terrace began. Bricks from the original fireplace were used in the new one. (Garry Chater photo)

Two Historic Railways

The sound of freight trains rumbling through the night, whistles wailing nostalgically like those of old steam engines, can still be heard in View Royal. They travel up and down Vancouver Island two or three times a week on the Esquimalt and Nanaimo Railway tracks, built by coal baron Robert Dunsmuir and his American partners in 1887.

Three British Columbians, including Dr. Helmcken, went to Ottawa to negotiate terms of Confederation in 1870-71 and were promised a railway as part of the deal. Victorians assumed that the transcontinental would continue to Vancouver Island by way of a bridge from the mainland, as approved by order in council of June 7, 1873. It was inconceivable that the industrial heart of the province, with its mines and mills, not to mention the naval base at Esquimalt and the civilized city of Victoria, would be left out.

When the Island line was dropped there was talk of secession. Delegations went to Ottawa and Premier Amor de Cosmos took the problem straight to the Imperial Government in London. All to no avail. The line would end on the mainland. Gastown won and grew up to become Vancouver.

Easterners didn't care about the Island railway. A San Francisco company was interested but American-controlled investment was frowned upon. Then Prime Minister Sir John A. Macdonald, by this time elected MP for Victoria in a byelection after a defeat in King-

ston, had a thought.[25] Robert Dunsmuir needed transportation for coal from his profitable Island mines - perhaps he might be persuaded? He was, with a little help from Ottawa in the form of a generous land grant. The Esquimalt and Nanaimo Railway was born April 28, 1884, with Robert Dunsmuir as president, Charles F. Crocker of San Francisco as vice-president, and Charles E. Pooley of Esquimalt as secretary.

Work was carried out with admirable efficiency on all sections of the line, which was completed in little more than a year. Construction on the southern portion began March 5, 1885, with blasting for the first rock cut, known as the Dunsmuir Cut near the head of Portage Inlet.

Well into the 1920s people took the train into town for shopping or visiting, returning in the evening. Promotional material for a 1912 View Royal subdivision claimed transportation to town was no problem as the E.&N. Railway was "within hail."

The View Royal section served several businesses, including the Atkins brothers' lime quarries. A letter dated March 9, 1899, confirms a contract with Atkins Brothers Silica Lime Brick Company for installation of a spur track approximately at the present boundary between View Royal and Langford.

E.&N. traffic Manager George L. Courtney wrote acknowledging receipt of $100 "as a guarantee that they

---

25 Or was it the Governor General, the Marquis of Lorne? An 1891 publication, *Victoria, the Queen City*, published under the auspices of the Corporation of the City of Victoria says "... the late Hon. Robert Dunsmuir having, at the suggestion of the Marquis of Lorne, then Gov. General, and other prominent persons, consented to assume the responsibility" for construction of the railway. The writer adds that "to build and equip the road, whose total length is 78 miles, cost over $2,940,000"

shall ship not less than one thousand barrels of lime in cars of the Esquimalt & Nanaimo Railway Company from Atkins Siding between this and the first day of June, 1899. Under which conditions this Company agrees to place a switch in the said siding for the above purpose." The Atkins company met its agreement and the deposit was returned.

Towards the end of World War I Burns Meats of Alberta built a slaughterhouse near the rail line west of Helmcken Road. Cattle were shipped from Alberta. The Chung family bought the business in 1948 from the second owner, Mr. Hubbard. They operate the only fully inspected slaughterhouse in the area, but no longer use the railway for transporting livestock.

Robert Dunsmuir's son James, then premier and soon to be lieutenant-governor of British Columbia, sold the line, including the land grant, to the Canadian Pacific Railway (CPR) in 1905. Robert's widow and others applied to the court for an injunction to prevent the sale. James's eldest son Robin, who thought the railway was being sold too cheaply, tried to raise money to buy it himself. His grand scheme was to bring timber down the Island by train to Portage Inlet, dredge a canal through to Esquimalt Harbour and float the logs through to mills. He was somewhat undercapitalized when he offered to put up a modest $250,000 of his own money if the president of the Great Northern Railway Company, James J. Hill, would provide the remaining $2,000,000 for the railway and the land. There is no record of a reply - and so another Portage Inlet/Esquimalt Harbour canal project floundered.

VIA Rail now operates the Dayliner passenger service. Canadian Pacific, which still owns the tracks, bills VIA for their use, and runs the reduced freight service. VIA has no mandate to provide commuter service, so the stretch of tracks linking Langford and Victoria cannot be used to alleviate automobile traffic problems. Some level of government could pay for the use of the tracks, but would have to buy its own rolling stock, pay CPR crews and maintenance. Supporters of a light rapid transit system suggest this would be cheaper, and more environmentally friendly than costly upgrading of the highway system for more automobile traffic.

ESQUIMALT & NANAIMO RAILWAY.			
SOUTH BOUND (Read Up.)			
STATIONS.	Miles from Wellingt'n	No 1. PASSENGER DAILY.	No. 3. PASSENGER Saturday.
		P. M.	P. M.
Victoria...............	78	Ar. 12.20	Ar. 7 00
Russell's.............	77	" 12.16	" 6.55
Esquimalt............	74	" 12.06	" 6.48
Stewart's.............	73	" 12.03	" 6.45
Parson's Bridge.....	72	" 12.00	" 6.42
Langford.............	70	" 11.53	" 6.36
Goldstream..........	67	" 11.43	" 6.27
Summit Siding......	58	" 11.15	" 6.00
Shawnigan Lake....	50	" 10.50	" 5.40
Cobble Hill.........	47	" 10.40	" 5.32
McPherson's.........	43	" 10.25	" 5.23
Koksilah.............	40	" 10.15	" 5.16
DUNCAN'S	38	**"10.10**	**" 5.12**
Somenos.............	35	" 10.00	" 5.05
Westholme...........	31	" 9.53	" 4.56
Chemainus...........	26	" 9.38	" 4.45
Oyster Bay Siding..	19	" 9.20	" 4.27
Oyster Bay..........	16	" 9.11	" 4.18
Alexandra Mine.....	10	" 8.58	" 4.00
Nanaimo.............	5	" 8.40	" 3.45
Wellington..........		De. 8.20 A. M.	De. 3.30 P. M.

Undated photo of steam train near Burns meat packing plant. (MacLachlan collection)

Old E.&N. timetables show two stations, Stewart's and Parson's Bridge, which no longer exist. Stewart's is thought to have been near the present Palmer Station where a spur line served the meat packing plant. Parson's would have been behind the Six-Mile House. (MacLachlan collection)

The long trestle over Price's field, looking north from Brydon Road, is filled in now. It runs from the Thetis Lake overpass between the Trans Canada Highway and Atkins Road. A construction camp and headquarters of the contractors, A. J. McLellan and Thomas Earle, were near this section, approximately where Atkins Road curves to join Highway 1A. (BCARS 65726)

Part of the 1,600-foot trestle seen from the harbour. Scowloads of timber were hauled up from a landing near Parson's Bridge to a works yard where carpenters prepared the trestle bents or bridge sections. (BCARS 64503)

Gangs of Chinese labourers moved loose rock north from this blasting for fill to the approaches of a 500-foot pile bridge over a small bay where Deadman's Creek joins the Portage Inlet. It joined a finished trestle 600 feet long, which The Daily Colonist described as this "most excellent piece of work ... strongly built of magnificent timber, well bolted and on a solid foundation." From this bridge, alongside the present View Royal Elementary School, the grade was pushed through to Price's Field below the present junction of the Trans-Canada and Highway 1A. (BCARS 95519)

Four men in black hats fish from the railway bridge near Deadman's Creek, ca. 1900. (BCARS 64476)

Engine No. 2 heading into town north of the rock cut where Atkins Road narrows between the E.&N. and the CN tracks. Beyond the cut was another trestle 1,800 feet long, now filled in with an overpass where Chilco Road narrows to a one-lane tunnel under the tracks. Yet another trestle crossed 'Mackenzie's field.' The last trestle in View Royal, 1,000 feet long, led to a 300-foot rock cut which brought the grade to Millstream, crossed by yet another trestle beyond the View Royal boundary. (BCARS 95520)

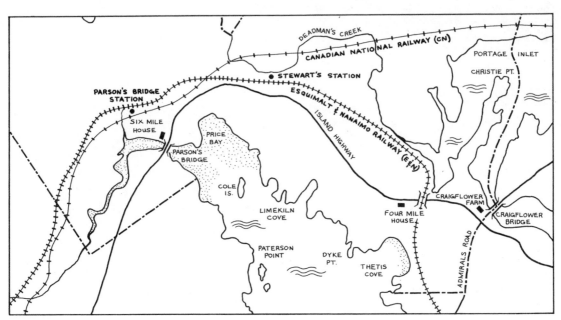

Map shows the two railways running parallel through View Royal, except where the CN passes under the E.&N. at the Thetis Lake underpass.

The Galloping Goose

There are no trains now on the Canadian National Railway (CN) tracks where logging trains and a gas-powered passenger train known as the Galloping Goose used to run daily. Most of the tracks between Victoria and Sooke have been taken up and the right-of-way is now the Galloping Goose trail, part of a regional linear park.

Construction of the line was begun by Canadian Northern Pacific in 1911, and dedicated in September, 1918.[26] The September 9 edition of the Victoria Daily Times reported that Canadian Northern Railway locomotive No. 1018 left the temporary Alpha Street Station for a 40-minute ride to end of steel with four coachloads of dignitaries. A terminal at Point Ellice

was completed in 1920 after Canadian National took over, and regular passenger service began in August, 1922.

The daily passenger service between Victoria and Sooke, inaugurated October 14, 1922, was used by local residents and businessmen for a few years. They travelled on a 30-passenger gas car powered by a Reo gasoline engine and equipped with a small baggage and mail compartment. The 'train' was operated by one man who served as engineer, conductor and trainman.

By 1924 a twice-weekly freight train and two or three heavy log trains a day were required to handle the increasing traffic from logging operations after the line was extended to Cowichan. One large source of freight was the scrap cordwood from the mills used as a domestic fuel until the 1950s. It was carried to Victoria in old boxcars with the roofs removed for easy loading.

The last train on the CN tracks was known as 'Victoria's Own Cannonball' - a vintage steam engine with two coaches chugging between Helmcken Road and the trestle over Millstream in the summers of 1969 and 1970. This stretch of track was leased and operated as a tourist attraction under the name of the Victoria Pacific Railway.

When the old engine was hauled up from its temporary station at 10 Atkins Road after its final run, Canadian National quickly abandoned the line.

'Victoria's Own Cannonball' with cowcatcher in a rock cut at the end of its brief stint as a tourist attraction in 1970. (Photo and souvenir pass from MacLachlan collection)

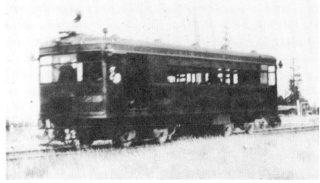

CNR motor coach #15810 heading out of Victoria in 1926. (MacLachlan collection)

---

26 Robert Turner of the Royal B.C. Museum has given permission to use excerpts from his book *Vancouver Island Railways*, published by Golden West Books, San Marino, California, 1973.

Lime Kilns And Brick Works

Pre-20th century industry in View Royal included brickworks as well as lumbering. Limestone quarries on Atkins Road and Hart Road supported commercial production for many years after Kenneth McKenzie found limestone for his Craigflower Farm brick-making.[27]

The first commercial enterprise may have been that of F. Richard and Company who advertised in the Colonist on June 8, 1859:

> NOTICE: THE SUBSCRIBERS having leased from the Government those extensive Lime Quarries in the vicinity of Craig Flower, would respectfully inform the public that they are now prepared to deliver lime to any part of the city at reasonable rates. All orders left at Mr. W. P. Saywood's or Messrs. Lester and Gibbs, will be thankfully received and promptly attended to.

Mention of a commercial, but apparently not too reliable, brickworks was found in a letter dated May 4, 1882, from the engineer superintending construction of the first naval drydock in Esquimalt. He reported to the chief commissioner of Lands and Works in Victoria on lack of progress at Mason's brickyard near Parson's Bridge:

> Sir: I have the honor to inform you that nothing has been done in the way of dock construction since I reported to you on the 22nd of April that the work was then at a standstill and had been so since the 12th of April. The waste of the present fine weather in

> forwarding the progress of the work is I consider most deplorable.
> I visited the Brickyard at Parson's Bridge on 1st May and found a few Chinamen employed making bricks. They informed me they commenced doing so on 28th April. I was told they are engaged by Mr. S. Gillespie, but the class of bricks they were turning out is a very poor one. Whether the bricks are intended for use in the dock or not I do not know.

The Atkins Brothers Silica Lime Brick Company quarries were busy enough by 1899 to justify a spur line from the E.&N. railway off Atkins Road to transport the product to other brickyards. MacLachlan identifies the Atkins spur as starting about where the tracks cross Atkins Road near the View Royal/Langford boundary.

A Capital Regional District manuscript (no source is attributed) mentions another company formed in 1906, operating at or near the Atkins siding. The directors of the Silica Brick and Lime Company were H. B. Thomson, J. Kingham and R. W. Clark. The plant was installed by contractor George H. Bradbury, an expert in the manufacture of sand-lime brick. It was built against a hill of sand in the middle of a large limestone bed. Water for the sand and lime mixture was brought by a flume from Thetis Lake. The same source says the railway spur ran under the hillside along a platform where the dried bricks from the retorts were loaded onto small cars.

---

27 According to a CRD manuscript McKenzie's quarry was on Helmcken Road. Remains of an old kiln were found during blasting of the rock behind Henry Louie's grocery at the corner of Helmcken and the Old Island Highway. The bay at the foot of Helmcken Road, two blocks away from this site, was once known as Limekiln Cove.

Beginnings Of Suburbia
"Select Homes by the Sea"

As bedroom suburbs go, View Royal is a late-comer.

In colonial days residential Victoria spread out around the fort to cover the farms of James Bay and Hillside as early as the 1850s and 60s. Some grand homes appeared in Esquimalt and on both sides of the Gorge in the 1880s and 90s, including several Dunsmuir extravaganzas, but 19th-century development stopped more or less at Esquimalt village.

In 1912 the population in the northern part of View Royal was large enough to support a new Anglican Church at Strawberry Vale, but the land south of the Sooke Road (Old Island Highway) was still largely farms and forest.

Victoria, however, had been in one of its boom periods for more than five profitable years. It was reasonable to suppose that the sheltered waterfront on the north side of Esquimalt Harbour would be the next logical place for summer homes or permanent residence.

The directors of the Island Investment Company were confident. Messrs. D. C. Reid, T. Reading and R. Foxhall and Captain E. Butler bought 80 acres from Dr.

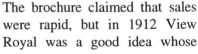

Dr. James Douglas Helmcken sold his View Royal waterfront property to a land development company in 1912. (BCARS 51777)

James Helmcken (part of the land his father bought in the 1850s) and engaged in vigorous promotion of the subdivision they named View Royal.

Facing up optimistically to a few drawbacks, the promoters promised graded roads, telephones, electricity and streetcars "within the season." Streetcars never came near the place, but Esquimalt streetcars were "within 20 minutes by launch." The E.&N. Railway was "within hail," and the C.N. Railway "must come within a stone's throw."

Other claims were premature. Mrs. Riley, one of the early buyers, had to pay to bring water from the highway. Subsequent owners paid Mrs. Riley a fee for the privilege of hooking into her water line.

Minor quibbles indeed, when the Island Investment Company was certain that "... mercantile advantages of such a port especially as it lies directly in the road of the increased traffic that will come with the opening of the Panama Canal, must be patent to the observing." But not very interesting to the few who bought for country living.

The brochure claimed that sales were rapid, but in 1912 View Royal was a good idea whose time had not come. The boom turned into a depression in 1913, and war came in 1914. Four years later migration patterns turned eastward when Oak Bay became the socially correct locale and Esquimalt went into a decline.

By the early 1920s several modest houses had been built along the View Royal Avenue waterfront but most of the fields and forest remained. The Depression brought another small influx in the 1930s when waterfront lots sold for as little as $500. Slowly, the central part of View Royal was built up and the old Stewart farm disappeared.

Other developers saw the potential in the 1930s and 40s. The Terry family, owners of the famous tea room and ice cream parlour on Douglas Street, sold the land they had bought from Helmcken descendants in 1929 to Geoff Newstead. Soon their vegetable farm at the end of View Royal Avenue gave way to building lots.

The prophecies of the 1912 brochure have been more than fulfilled, except for the mercantile aspect which

no true View Royalite would countenance. The only residential waterfront property on Esquimalt Harbour is within View Royal. Portage Inlet and every creek and stream provide more 'waterfront' lots, no longer at bargain prices.

Lateblooming suburbia has caught up, price-wise, to most other 'desirable' residential property in Greater Victoria. Here is a brief price comparison:

1850s:	J. S. Helmcken - $5 an acre
1860s:	Cooperville - 3 waterfront lots, $50
1912:	Subdivision, $600 and up ¼ acre ($2,400 per acre)
1933:	waterfront lot, $500
1992:	waterfront lot, $200,000
1993:	waterfront home listed at $800,000

Impressive homes on Helmcken's "unploughable" rocks. (Robert Duffus photo)

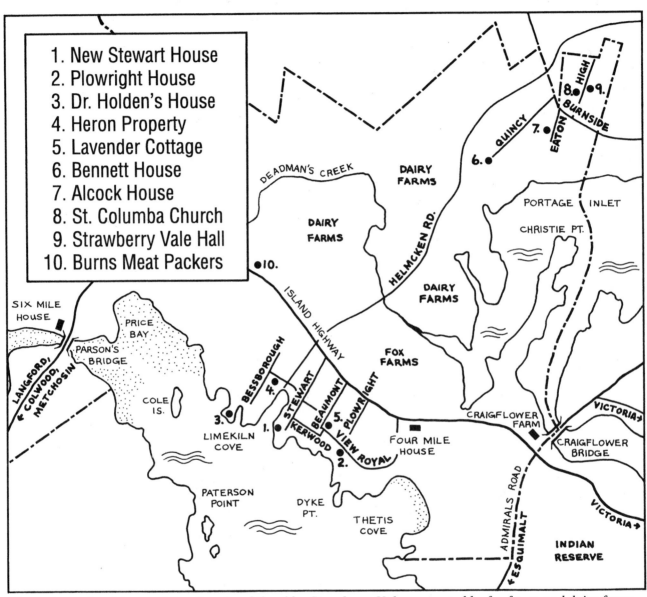

1. New Stewart House
2. Plowright House
3. Dr. Holden's House
4. Heron Property
5. Lavender Cottage
6. Bennett House
7. Alcock House
8. St. Columba Church
9. Strawberry Vale Hall
10. Burns Meat Packers

The main roads of the new View Royal and the older Strawberry Vale, separated by fox farms and dairy farms.

Stories And Reminiscences

A selection of personal recollections of View Royal chosen to represent the three older neighbourhoods: the harbourfront, Strawberry Vale and the far side of Parson's Bridge.

From a brochure extolling the virtues of the 1912 subdivision of part of the Helmcken property.

The Fisher house on Heddle Avenue, one of the early houses in the new subdivision (Alice King collection)

Fishing In Deadman's Creek

Ruth McTavish Pearce
(a great grand-daughter of Dr. J. S. Helmcken)

Young Ruth McTavish and her brother John photographed with their catch from Deadman's Creek, part of the family property. (Photo courtesy Ruth McTavish Pearce)

My memories of View Royal go back to the early 20s. My Uncle Jack, John A. McTavish, owned the property from the water to the Old Island Highway which now includes Tovey Crescent, Prince Robert Drive and the end of View Royal Avenue.

He had a home on the point, opposite Dr. Holden's house, and we spent many happy days visiting there, playing on White Shell Beach, climbing the hill in spring to pick wildflowers, lilies, lady slippers and buttercups. Heddle Avenue up the hill was named for Uncle Jack's sister Dorothy who married Edwin Heddle.

My dad, Duncan McTavish, owned the land on the other side of the highway where he had a farm.

John Bate and his family lived there and looked after the farm. I don't remember what he grew, but I do remember that he had five pigs named Matthew, Mark, Luke, John and Ruth - my brother's name is John. When we went out to visit the farm Mrs. Bate always treated us to a very special tea!

Another brother, Claus S. McTavish, owned property from the farm back to the railroad. My brother and I caught many little fish in Deadman's Creek.

The farm was eventually sold to the Alexander family who built a large house, Chantecler, which was run as a roadhouse. The replica of Fort Victoria is there now.

Deadman's, or Craigflower, Creek in winter with Gull Road houses in the background. (Robert Duffus photo)

Uncle Jack died in 1929 and his property was sold to Mr. Terry who owned Terry's Drug Store, and he in turn sold it to Mr. Newstead whose company then developed the area.

In 1949 our family came back to View Royal when my dad and mother bought their house on Plowright Road. It was originally a summer cottage but had been added to over the years. They had two lots, one of which they gave my husband and me, where we built our home in 1956. Many happy years were spent in View Royal. We rented Mr. Pegg's house at the top of the Four Mile Hill for four years before we built, and over the years Bob and I were involved in many community activities. Bob was with the volunteer fire department for 30 years, 10 as a fireman and 20 as a trustee, which my dad had also been.

Our daughter carried on the View Royal tradition when she and her husband enlarged my parents' house and lived there until 1988. We moved in 1985.

The McTavish farm where the writer visited Mr. and Mrs. John Bate. The house stood on the site of the old roadhouse called Chantecler, later Fort Victoria R.V. Park. (McTavish collection)

Remembering Craigflower Country

the late Duncan Douglas McTavish, 1953

Ruth Pearce contributed a short memoir written by her father after he retired to his home on Plowright Road in 1949. He was the grandson of Dr. John Sebastian Helmcken and Cecilia Douglas Helmcken, and great-grandson of James and Amelia Douglas.

Going back about an even hundred years there wasn't much in the area we now know as View Royal, except that part at the corner of Admirals Road and Craigflower Road, which was developed by the Hudson's Bay Company through their agricultural section which operated as The Puget's Sound Agricultural Company.

In my younger days the Craigflower property was the home of the John Parker family, and Mr. Parker operated a slaughterhouse on the west side of the road, adjoining the Admirals Road corner. There was no sanitary arrangement at that time around a slaughterhouse, and any time you drove past the place you were well advised to keep a good heavy handkerchief to your nose. This perfume was often spoken of as Parker's Attar of Roses.

Carrying on toward the present View Royal, the next property was the Four Mile House. The Calverts must have had considerable acreage as they went right down to the water on Esquimalt Harbour and north to Deadman's River, across the present [Old Island] highway.

Next we come to what we now know as View Royal and this property from the Four Mile Hill to Parson's

Bridge and north to the Burnside road, the whole length of Helmcken Road, was owned by my grandfather Dr. J. S. Helmcken.

The part of the property, say from Plowright Road to Helmcken Road, south of the highway was what we knew in the old days as Stewart's farm, as Mr. Stewart, the father of our grand old lady of View Royal, Amy Stewart, leased the land from Dr. Helmcken and farmed it.

In the old days we used to go to Esquimalt by tram-car and have a boatman there (probably Sammy Doncas-

Indian woman gathering clams on View Royal Beach, photographed by Duncan McTavish, ca. 1910.

ter) row us across to Stewart's to spend a day or afternoon at the farm, and afterwards take us back to Esquimalt to catch the car. In later years, of course, we used motor boats. The Stewarts were grand people and many a good time we had at their farm.

The end of this little journey is Parson's Bridge and the Six Mile House. The bridge was named after Mr. Parson who lived there in the very early days. Later on the roadhouse was run by the Price family, and it too was a popular roadside resort. It was quite a way from town in the early days when travel was restricted to horse and buggy or wagon transportation.

That would be about the limit of what we knew as the Craigflower country. As to what we now know as View Royal: this was developed by Dr. J. D. Helmcken, having been given to the doctor by his father Dr. J. S. Helmcken, and consisted of that part lying between Plowright Road and Helmcken Road, and bounded on the north by Deadman's River.

The adjoining part, from Helmcken Road to the end of View Royal Avenue, was eventually sold to Geoff Newstead, and the piece across the road where Morrow Court now stands [Fort Victoria] was sold in the early 20s to the Alexanders who built the Chantecler and operated it for some time.

Since the twenties View Royal has grown into the most beautiful suburb of the most beautiful city in Canada, through the efforts of the residents who have some of the finest gardens to be found in any part of the Victoria district. The View Royal Garden Club which was started some few years ago does all it can to foster the development and beautification of the district and has a goodly number of enthusiastic members on its membership list. [Ed. note: True in 1993 as it was 40 years ago when this was written. Mr. McTavish was president of the garden club for six years.]

Mr. and Mrs. Duncan McTavish in their garden on Plowright Road after he retired from his brokerage and insurance business in 1949. He was a Victoria alderman for over a decade from the late 1930s. (McTavish collection)

Camping At Aunt Amy's

Amy Lillian (Stewart) Culling
(from an interview taped by Shoreline School students)

Ninety-six year old Mrs. Culling is a granddaughter of James Stewart of Seaview Farm. She lives in the house Amy Stewart built in 1913.

My father was born at Craigflower farm shortly after my grandparents came here in 1853.[28] They came out on the *Norman Morison* with the McKenzies. My mother was a Parker who also lived at Craigflower. So both grandparents came out on the

The house Amy Stewart built near the end of Stewart Avenue in 1913. (Michael Pope collection)

Norman Morison, mother's people from Kent, England, and dad's from Scotland.

I first visited View Royal as a child when we came to camp on my aunt's farm in 1905. There were quite a few people camping around here then. We came out as soon as school closed and stayed until Labour Day. Other children were my cousin Isabel Stewart and her brother Harley, who was older and worked around the farm. It was all a big field then. Later, after the war, my parents bought a house near here.

I remember we always had boats. When I was eight years old my father bought a flat-bottomed boat with four oars, so we got quite a lot of people in. We took our picnics to White Beach, and up to Spring Beach, between Plowright and Beaumont. There were big tubs there, filled by a spring, and the cows would drink water from it.

My cousin had an inboard motor boat and took us picnicking around to the lagoon and the islands where we would catch crabs off the rocks. We went over to Magazine Island when there was no one there, and ran through all the places where they used to keep the powder. Our voices would echo in the empty buildings. Later the Hetheringtons came and lived in the

---

28 The Robert Melrose Diary notes that "Mrs. Stewart gave birth to a male child" on Saturday, February 19, 1853. "Voltaire born 1694," the diarist adds.

house facing the harbour, a nice home with lots of glass. They had lots of flowers gone wild, bachelor buttons and nasturtiums which we used to pick, and an awful lot of parsley.

There was once a boat which took people back and forth pulled by a rope running from the island to the shore on this side of the harbour. The navy came here a lot, and Aunt Amy supplied the island with milk and cream from the farm.

A naval lieutenant was a great friend of my aunt. The navy people used to come to hunt around here when it was all bush up as far as the highway. That's how he met Aunt Amy. He wanted to marry her and take her to England, but the family didn't think she should leave, and Aunt Amy's mother wasn't well at the time, nor was her father. Her father died in 1892 and mother in 1902, so she took over the farm when they died. I still have a plate, one of a set with all different flowers, that the lieutenant gave her before he left.

Amy Stewart as a beautiful young lady when she was courted by a naval officer, ca. 1890. (BCARS 4119)

The Heron Family And Friends

Alice (Heron) King

These are some notes about 1920s View Royal as I remember it, being only five and a half years old when we moved from our farm at Pine Lake, Alberta.

Why did we come to View Royal? My mother's sister Henrietta, always called Aunt Hetta, lived on Cole Island where her husband, Harry Hetherington, was in charge of the ammunition stored in the sheds. He had previously been in the North West Mounted Police, but had been on the island during the First World War.

When we arrived my mother, my 13-year old sister Molly and I spent a few days in the cottage next to the Plowrights on View Royal Avenue. We could hear the Indian powwows on the beach across the harbour.

My father, Robert Heron, and 15-year-old brother Arthur came to View Royal a week or so after us, having settled the sale of the farm at Pine Lake. He bought the house and property on View Royal Avenue where we lived until 1929. The land extended from the foot of Helmcken Road along the bay, northwest on View

The gate at the end of View Royal Avenue, where Bessborough now crosses, kept the Stewarts' cows from wandering into the bog. (Alice King collection)

Arthur Heron and friend on the tennis court near the end of View Royal Avenue (Alice King collection)

Royal Avenue to Bessborough Road. The property consisted of rocks covered with moss and spring-blooming plants, and some arable patches of soil.

Some areas were covered with clamshells where we found Indian arrowheads and other shaped rocks which were given to the museum by our friend Reverend Robert Connell whose hobby was natural history. He was one of the founders of the Victoria Natural History Society.

There was a spring and a boggy area on View Royal Avenue where stray cattle sometimes became mired, so it became necessary for the road to be closed off with fences and gates at Helmcken and Bessborough. As time went on our garden consisted of a tennis court, grass, fruit trees, berries, vegetables and flowers.

West of our property was a wonderful world of trees, rocks, beaches, flowers and shrubs, many acres bordered by the Palmer property, Gibraltar, on the west and the McTavish property. They gave us permission to walk through this acreage, which was a shortcut to Palmer station to catch the train in the early morning to shop or visit in Victoria and return in late afternoon.

Other transportation to Victoria was by jitney or the Veterans Stage run by Mr. Wale from Langford or Happy Valley. Both made two trips to Victoria and back every day, and the fare in the early 20s was 15 cents each way. Vehicles still drove on the left side of the road then. The highway was cement.

The Stewarts leased a large tract of land which had originally been owned by Dr. J. S. Helmcken and farmed by Mr. Stewart Senior from the 1860s. Miss Amy Stewart and her brother John ran a few Jersey cows which supplied the Stewarts with butter and the few nearby residents with lard pails of Jersey milk with cream on top and skim milk for drinking.

We fetched our own milk each day and always had a little chat with Miss Stewart who always gave us a cookie, a real treat. At Christmas we were given a tiny slice of her plum pudding which we had watched each day cooking in a copper boiler over coals in her garden.

Old Luk, her Chinese helper on the farm, was tolerant of children and generous with lichi nuts and Chinese lilies for mother at Chinese New Year. There was a

large hay field where children did not play, or they would be lectured by Johnny Stewart.

Joe Stewart, Amy's brother, and his family camped on adjacent property. This is the only place I have ever seen where a huge patch of yellow paintbrush bloomed each spring. It was destroyed when the seaplane business took over.

Miss Stewart subdivided the property between the house fence on Stewart Avenue and View Royal Avenue, and the Jim Pilgrims were the first to build there. The Dan Stewarts had property at the corner of View Royal Avenue and Stewart and had a summer house there. The Diments built next to them. Their sons Gil and Fred, in their teens, were fond of swimming and diving off rafts in the bay, and tolerant of slightly younger children joining them. Their sister, Doris Hawthorne, later lived nearby.

Lavender Cottage at the corner of View Royal Avenue and Beaumont was empty when we first came but was bought some time in the mid-20s by Mr. and Mrs. Dudley Colclough who were also from Pine Lake, Alberta. Their son Pat often played tennis on our court. Mr. Colclough used to swim every morning off the rocks at the foot of Beaumont in the chilly water.

Our neighbours included the Stevensons on the corner of Helmcken and View Royal. His son Jack was my age and there was a baby, Fred. When they moved the Drummond-Hays moved in. Elderly Mrs. Drummond-Hay, her daughters Amy and Harriet were friends, and a son Ted was a very good tennis player. He insisted

Seaplanes flew to Seattle and Vancouver from a dock, still noted on maps, on Dan Stewart's property at Helmcken Bay. (Duncan McTavish photo)

on playing even when his doctor forbade it, and died on our court a few years after their arrival.

Harriet and her husband lived there for several years. They had a ram, George, tethered on the road allowance - woe betide you if you got close enough for him to bunt you! They eventually moved away to raise sheep elsewhere. In 1929 or 1930 Captain and Mrs. Johnston and daughter Jean moved in. Mrs. Boden built between the corner property and the Drummond-Hays opposite our tennis court. She raised a few Togenberg goats during the few years she was there. The next owners, the Sherringhams, stayed for several years. Other families who came to the area later were the Sheards, to the foot of Stewart Avenue, and the Rileys.

Bessborough Avenue was opened up by the highways department in the early 1920s when Dr. and Mrs. Holden built at the foot of the road on a rocky promontory. Dr. Holden often gave me a ride to school and my brother to Victoria where he worked in the Imperial Bank of Canada. Dr. Holden was on the plane that flew from Lansdowne airfield to Seattle and crashed in September, 1928. It was one of the first flights.

Electricity was not available until the late 20s, as the B.C. Electric required 10 residents to pay a set sum, $10 per month, before they would consider putting in a line. Telephones came later, there was still no phone when we left in 1929. Water was supplied by the Victoria Water Board, and apparently it was only a matter of having a water meter installed and water piped to the house. Mail to R.R.#1, Victoria, was delivered five or six days a week.

There was no school in View Royal so we went to the four-room Craigflower School, which was pulled down a few years ago, for Grades 1 to 8 then to Victoria High. A school bus picked up pupils from Thetis Lake Road and along the highway and brought us back in the afternoon. I remember two Barkers, two or three Rants, three Wilmshursts, one Alexander and one Heron (me!). Before the bus we often had rides in passing cars or wood trucks. The older Alexander boys always stopped, and were great teases.

Although we did not live in Saanich, pupils attended Saanich schools and so school taxes went to Saanich. There were frequent discussion groups at our house about the total cost of running Craigflower School, led by Dr. H. A. Francis whose Burnside Road acreage bordered on Saanich. He claimed that the tax dollars collected by Saanich amounted to more than the total cost of running Craigflower school.

His large property bordered on Burnside, the CN railway and Deadman's Creek. When my aunt and uncle

Alice Heron's parents bought a former Rant home, Beverley, now the site of storage sheds where Burnside enters the highway. (Alice King collection)

retired from Cole Island they built a house on five acres of his land, with railway, creek and Creed Road boundaries.[29] After Uncle Harry died my parents moved there and ran a few milk cows. A few years later they bought the old Rant house 'Beverley,' where Burnside Road enters the highway. The property extended to the creek and along the railway track to Palmer Station. There was a good orchard - now it is the site of storage sheds! The Fishers had lived there previously, and Mrs. Fisher later built elsewhere in View Royal.

After moving about the province [as a public health nurse] I returned to Victoria in 1958 and eventually settled at 296 View Royal Avenue, and lived there happily until I married in 1964. I would move back if the house were available!

View of Craigflower, ca. 1908, from a drawing by Reverend Robert Connell. (Alice King collection)

---

29 Harry Arthur Francis, surgeon, of Brookside Farm, Parson's Bridge, trained at St. Bartholomew's Hospital in England. He bought 100 acres in the Burnside area from the Hudson's Bay Company in 1905 or 1906. He was married to Louisa Gascoigne. Their daughter Phyllis, lived on part of the property until her death in 1988 at the age of 99.

The Bennetts Of Quincy Street

Louise Baur

My grandparents lived at 20 Quincy Street for many years.

Fred Bennett came from Northwold, a tiny village near Sandringham Castle in Norfolk, England. He trained as a horticulturist in the nurseries and green-houses of the royal residence, but left his work and his parents for Canada in 1888 when he was in his early 20s. His dream was to own his own land.

During the voyage from Plymouth to Montreal he met Maria Manly-Brooke, also travelling to Montreal with her widowed mother and three sisters. Maria's dream was to move as far west as one could go and live beside the Pacific Ocean.

Fred and Maria, known as Minnie, were married three years later. They moved to Lachine, Quebec, where Fred established his second green-house business. In 1905, at Maria's gentle and persistent urging, Fred sold the business and launched into yet another venture in the rough tent city of Edmonton. His carnations and roses were not in demand as they had been in sophisti-cated Montreal, but onions, tomatoes and cucumbers were, and the business flour-ished.

Edmonton was the wrong side of the Rockies for Maria. The family arrived in Victo-

Mr. and Mrs. Fred Bennett. (Louise Baur collection)

ria on July 1, 1910. Fred was a nurseryman at Woodward's Greenhouses, where the Fairfield Plaza is now. They lived in a rented cottage on the shores of Foul Bay, so Maria's dream was fulfilled as she taught her four children to swim, picked berries, baked bread, swept the sand out of her house - and sang in St. Matthias choir.

But Fred still wanted his own land, something nearly impossible to achieve in England. A few years later they bought several acres in View Royal. The property stretched from Quincy Street to Eaton Avenue, and from Burnside to the E.&N. railway tracks.

They lived in an amazing house, built before the turn of the century by a Mr. Pease. It was said that he had built another exactly like it in Oak Bay. The house was long and low, with six bedrooms (three with fireplaces), rooms for servants, a 'back kitchen' with scullery and skylights and swinging doors, and one enormous bathroom. Every wall was insulated with sheets of cork. The back kitchen was enormous and useless as a kitchen, so Grandfather Fred kept his pool table there. He was a whiz at snooker.

At last Fred Bennett had his own land, and the family was enchanted with the property. There were wild flowers and great oaks, and huge glacial rocks on the property. Fred built a sunken garden, a gazebo, rockeries and lovely gardens, and specialized in lilies.

The Pacific Ocean - at least Portage Inlet at the end of the Gorge waterway - was there for Maria, as was St. Columba Church and the choir. As children we loved to visit. Grandfather would show us the bees 'dancing' and how to watch them go in and out of the hive. "Don't bother them, and they won't bother you," he told us. Grandmother would serve tea as she would to adults, which made us feel we were special.

Fred Bennett died in 1948, and Maria in 1954, but the property remained with the family until the late 70s. The lovely oak trees are still there.

Their youngest daughter, my aunt Winona, who used to offer us rides around the garden on the wonderfully gentle Jersey cow Brownie, sent the following memories of old View Royal. She was about five years old when the family moved there, and retained an interest in the area as a real estate agent for many years.

Apples For The Trainmen

Winona McKeage

I remember the logging train went by every day, up in the morning and back at night. Old 1028 sometimes had only a single log on a flat car, higher than a man's head. I used to wave at the train when it went by and the trainmen would wave back. When the apples from our orchard were ripe, Dad packed a big box for me and when the old 1028 came along they stopped the train and took the apples.

One Christmas the train stopped and they blew the whistle, and when I went out they gave me a big box of chocolates. It was in three compartments and had a tiger skin cover. A few years ago I went to list an old house near Helmcken Road. The owner was an old man of 93. He said he had just had the monthly Railway letter and there was a piece in it about The Little Apple Girl. I told him he was looking at her.

The house my parents bought was built in 1897 by Mr. Pease, who had a German wife, and it was said it was built for German officers. When we went there you could see right over to Esquimalt Harbour. There were 12 rooms - room 13 was part of the old kitchen, which was large enough for a restaurant. There were small fireplaces in the three front rooms, but they didn't give out much heat. There were nearly two acres altogether. The family bought it for $500, with $50 down and $15 a month. Times have changed!

At the corner of Burnside and Holland Road was the Vickery and Fisher dairy. They had about 75 cows, mostly Holsteins. I remember the time Dad got home late and went to milk Pixie. She was usually tied on the lawn in front of the old house but when he took the bucket and sat down to milk he found it was the Holstein bull from the dairy. He said he very quickly backed away and called the dairy, and they were very glad to get their bull back. Our cow Brownie came from there. She was Jersey and milking Shorthorn, and lived to the age of 30. Charlie Fisher was known as Cow Fisher, and his brother Percy, who lived at the corner of Holland and Hastings, was Pig Fisher. Mr. Vickery hung himself but no-one knew for sure why.

Every school day I knew if I was late or not by where I met a big team of Clydes. The teamster always told me the time. He was hauling mash from the brewery for the cows.

Mrs. Gaunt lived alone in the house at the top of the hill. She was always dressed in heavy black and never went out except to church. Next was the old Bell house, and the Murrays' behind that. Maggie, the youngest girl, was full of fun. I remember the Hard Times dance. The girls had to make a dress costing not over a dollar. Maggie made one out of potato sacks, embroidered with wool and won first prize. My sisters made theirs of curtains and flour sacks.

On Helmcken Road on the right was the Swengers' house. They had a 300-acre dairy farm where Victoria General Hospital is now. When prices were low I couldn't sell it for $50,000. What would it be worth now! Farther down on the other side of the track where the Trans Canada Highway is now, on what is now Centennial Park, was Tommy Mould's farm. He had the contract to kill and burn all the cattle diagnosed as having tuberculosis. We used to wonder how many went to the butcher shop.

Then on the right was Deadman's River, which seems to have a fancy name now. On the left before the Old Island Highway was the Red and Silver Fox farm, but as the Depression became worse it was impossible to sell the skins, and the owners couldn't afford to feed the animals. One night all the gates were opened and the foxes were set free. The Depression did some good anyway.

Children used to row across the Gorge to Craigflower School from our area. There used to be thousands of

THE BENNETT HOUSE

G. DURRANT '93

The Bennetts' home at the foot of Quincy Street had a clear view over Portage Inlet and The Pie, later called Christie Point. (Gladys Durrant drawing)

wild ducks on Portage Inlet, and black and white swans that came every winter.

There was an old house below the tracks that was haunted by a young man with blond wavy hair and a sweet smile, wringing his hands and seeming in great distress. When new people bought the house and floated it around the corner on Portage Inlet he was never seen again. We did know who he was, I've forgotten his name but I do remember seeing his ghost more than 70 years ago. The highway covers the place now.

Stancil Lane

Phyllis McAdams

Burnside Road was a cow trail when Ernest Stancil arrived in View Royal. Born in Winnipeg in 1891, Mr. Stancil came to Victoria with his parents in 1898. He worked on construction of Victoria buildings, and built many houses in Saanich and View Royal. He and his wife lived in 14 of the many houses Ernest built and sold, one of them at 14 Eaton Road.

Four of these were on a little roadway through an old chicken farm off Burnside Road, which they called Stancil Lane, named after his family and his wife whose maiden name was Lane. There were not many bulldozers around in those days or ditchdiggers. Septic tanks were dug with hand shovels and basements were excavated by horse and plough. Christie Point was a favourite picnic spot reached by rowing up the Gorge in a four-oar rowboat.

The Plowrights

Phyllis McAdams

William and Elsie Plowright came to the bush and parkland of View Royal soon after the new subdivision was put on the market in 1912. They began building their home on the waterfront property shortly after they were married in 1913.

Lumber for their house was brought from Victoria by horse team and wagon. When it was completed in 1915 water was supplied from a well and they had their own light plant. William made a lane from their home to the highway, which was then just a dirt road. The land ran along a fence on the eastern boundary of the Stewart farm and later became Plowright Road.

In the early days the nearest store was Crosby's grocery on Tillicum Road near the Gorge Road. Mr. Crosby delivered groceries by horse and cart.

When the Plowrights went into Victoria they rowed across the harbour to Esquimalt and took the E.&N.

train or the tram car into town. There was a footpath all along the waterfront to Esquimalt if they chose to walk, but this was a long way around.

Later a bus ran to Craigflower and Admirals Road. They looked on this as a great convenience, even though they had to walk along the muddy highway in gumboots. These they hid in bushes near the bus stop until they returned to walk back up the slippery hill.

They were building a new house further up the hill on Plowright Avenue when William, a music teacher who had his own music studio and band, was killed by a passing car one night when walking away from the bus stop at Craigflower. Elsie later moved into the unfinished new house, working in the garden she loved, until her death in 1966.

A truly regal lady, Elsie was born in Scotland in 1882 and came to Victoria with her parents James and

The Plowright house seen from the lower lawn of their neighbours, Lydia and Malcolm Morrison. Both gardens were terraced down to the sea, and both properties had small cottages near the waterfront. (Gladys Durrant drawing from a 1930s photograph)

Elsie Plowright with Snowball, one of her goats and neighbour's child by woods near Plowright Road. (Morrison album)

Annie Donaldson when she was six years old. She and her eight brothers and sisters went to the old Kingston Street and South Park Schools. As a young girl she went into training as a nurse, and later took a stenographic course. She and William had a son Charles and a granddaughter Pauline.

One of Elsie Plowright's brothers, John Donaldson, seeded an oyster bed near Parson's Bridge in 1908. The oysters were brought in by railway from the east.

To School In A Milk Van

Kathleen (Barker) McConnan

I have known View Royal since 1919 when father bought over 400 acres in the Highland district, along Thetis Lake Road. The Thetis Lake overpass was the site of a large Chinese vegetable garden.

I went to Craigflower School from 1923 to 1929, after three years at Strawberry Vale where I boarded with my grandparents. The school bus from the Six Mile House area was a milk van, with a covered roof and wire mesh sides, and planks for seats. We called it the Cootie Cage. After biking three miles on gravel road from Thetis Lake and picking up the bus on the highway, I often spent the first two classes standing over the large floor heat vent to dry out.

In 1929 the Victoria school board would not take any more Saanich pupils in Victoria High School - it was full! So from 1929 to 1932 the Saanich High School was held at Tolmie School and buses used to bring pupils from the outer regions. During those three years

Remains of original Craigflower Farm buildings photographed in 1931, much as young Kay Barker saw them on her way to school in the 1920s. (BCARS 95602)

75

Mount View, Mount Douglas and Mount Newton high schools were built.

I remember apple trees growing on both sides of the Four Mile Hill, and when we walked home from school the tallest boy had the job of reaching up for a delicious treat. At the corner of Craigflower and Admirals and the highway the old fences and pig pens of Craigflower Farm (where the motel is now) were still standing, and horses grazed in the fields across the road. There was a small store, grocery and post office owned by the Fulton family, and later by the Pringles. The stretch of Craigflower Road on the Portage Inlet side was still Hudson's Bay property, and very heavily timbered.

To go into town we took the Veterans Stages owned by Mr. Wale. They picked up passengers in the 700 block Yates Street, turned right on Douglas to the Gorge Road to View Royal and Langford. The stages were rather crowded at times and we would have to sit on someone's knee. Vancouver Island Coach Lines ran buses out the Gorge Road to the corner of Island Highway, Admirals and Craigflower roads. Veterans Stages could pick up passengers there, but not let them off.

In 1928 I stayed with a girl friend on View Royal Avenue at the foot of Helmcken, and we used to walk all around the waterfront. There were only a few houses, and cows grazed on the Stewart farm. Dr. Holden lived in a large house on the point at the end of Bessborough. A later owner, Mr. John Goldring, was kind enough to lend his place for garden parties by various groups.

The bungalow opposite Louie's Store, at the corner of the Island Highway and Helmcken Road, was the home of Frank White, a large rawboned logger, who cleared land between the highway and the railroad. Another large well-timbered piece of land between the highway and the railway, now Glenairlie, was logged by Fats Atkinson.[30] The land off Helmcken from the corner of Jedburgh to the underpass, where View Royal School is located, was a fox farm owned by a Mr. Hanson. He used a scythe to cut the thistles and

vetch that grew on the sides of the roads, to feed his stock and use as bedding.

The Four Mile House was home of the Gouge family, a favourite stopping place for horse and buggy en route up-island. During the 1939-45 war it was used for A.R.P. [Air Raid Precaution] meetings and home nursing classes. At one time it was a tea room run by a singer in the Sweet Adelines singing group who had a large collection of shoes in glass cases, from half an inch up in size and all materials - glass, wood and leather. There were many suggestions for the building but the dangerous turn from the highway was a drawback.

We were married in 1939 and moved to View Royal in 1940. Our street was two gravel roads then. The sign at the corner of Helmcken read Jedburgh and the one at the highway corner was Jedborough. You couldn't drive from one end to the other because there was no road bed to join the two ends. There was one house at one end and two at the other. We made it three in 1941.

Ainslie Helmcken, the late Victoria city archivist, remembered when the Helmcken land was sold and how he helped dig the ditch on Jedburgh when a boy. When my husband and I cleared our land we found old road beds of rock, just where we wanted a vegetable garden. Now the rocks have made a good foundation for our driveway.

Random Reminiscences

At the corner of Hemlcken and the highway (south side) was a small grocery store with a row of stools to serve coffee, two gas pumps out front and a small car repair shop at the side. Cy Parsons ran the repair shop and later had the Texaco station where the Medical Building is now. He married Amy who helped out in the store and served coffee. Across from this was King's Grocery and Gorman's Drug Store. At the northwest corner of Helmcken and the Island Highway Mr. Campbell's building housed a butcher shop, the Betty Ann Bakery and a barber shop. Across was a garage where Sammy's Chinese restaurant is today.

---

30 Streets around the present elementary school were named after the Atkinson children Suzanne, Glen and Brian when the area was developed after World War II.

I remember helping neighbours round up stray goats belonging to Mrs. Minifie on Beaumont Avenue. One time our son and dog and I went for a walk to Thetis Lake Park, at the time when work crews were building the new Trans Canada. We met Mama goat and her two fully-grown kids, and she took a hate for our dog, and started butting me to protect her kids. I grabbed her horns and told Jim and dog to run over the hill. Then I twisted her ears and while she was still shaking her head - I ran. Over the hill Jim was telling the men on the work site that Mummy was being attacked by a goat. And they were laughing! But when I appeared, puffing, covered with white goat hair and smelling like one, it was no longer a laughing matter. The goats had got out of their pen and wandered into the park, not for the first time.

I remember someone was killed on the highway at the corner of Jedburgh, and land was bought to straighten the dangerous bend. That was 40 years ago and we are still waiting for the road to be fixed.

During 1945-46 Constable Lockie of the B.C. Police started a Boys Club. He lived in the first house on the highway up from Stewart. Softball was organized, and two years later, when Lockie was moved, my husband Ted took over. He had great help from Indian Chief Percy Ross, who gave ground for a field within the reserve, and the Indian children played with the View Royal boys for another two years. Styles changed and softball went forward under Buzz Beasley when the Centennial Park on Helmcken Road came into being. Others who helped with the park were Mr. Flower, Marjorie Aldersmith, Ed Stancil, Jack Ross and Jim Barker. Flower and Barker planted the trees along the edge of the park.

I remember Don Ross had a farm at the corner of the highway and the present Burnett Road. He later moved and bought land next to the railroad, now Pheasant Lane and subdivision. And below him was MacLennan's dairy. During one New Year's dance at the Community Hall a call came that his farm was burning. All the men left on the firetruck which was in the same hall as the dance.

When war was declared with Japan Vancouver Island was considered a danger spot. The View Royal community hall was built especially for meetings, fire practice and home nursing courses, and arrangements for blackouts for windows were organised. Holding tanks were placed all over View Royal for the one firetruck housed at the hall. The holding tank on Jedburgh is next door to us and was built against a rock. It is still there but filled in now. Some of the people working on the project were Jim Pilgrim, Sam Bell, W. Benson, Mr. Harper, Mrs. Edna Bull, Mr. Palmer and myself. It was all done by volunteer labour. View Royal has changed since then from a quiet rural community to an area of subdivisions where fields used to be.

Gibraltar, the well-named Palmer House overlooking Esquimalt harbour. (Maureen Duffus photo)

View Royal Is My Home

Michael Pope

I was 14 when my maternal grandfather died in 1930. His estate was divided between his three daughters and, coming at the beginning of the Depression, it was a lifesaver to my parents who were trying to sell their home in Oak Bay and move to a smaller place.

In 1932 they 'found View Royal' and my mother used her inheritance to purchase two waterfront lots on Seymour Street (now Kerwood) for the princely sum of $500 each. My father and I built a small house on the property which became home to my mother, father, sister Judith and myself.

The house was directly across the road from the original farmhouse of the James Stewart family, who had operated Seaview Farm since 1862. Miss Amy Stewart, affectionately known as Aunt Amy, no longer lived in the farmhouse but in the house built for her in 1913 on Stewart Avenue near the corner of Kerwood.

The imitation log-siding house built by the writer and his father in 1932. (Michael Pope collection)

She still maintained a small farm bounded by Stewart, Kerwood and View Royal Avenue, where she kept cows and supplied the neighbourhood with milk. Amy Stewart was born in the farmhouse in 1870 and lived in View Royal for 93 years. She left Vancouver Island once, didn't like it, returned after three days and never left again. She died in 1963.

When we first moved here Kerwood Avenue did not continue on to Beaumont but stopped just past the farmhouse. When the public works department decided to extend the road through to Beaumont it was found that the old farmhouse was on the right of way and would have to be removed. Nowadays that would be no problem; it would be designated a heritage building and moved to a different site. Unfortunately the building was torn down in 1946 or '47, despite protests, and another part of View Royal's history was lost forever.

I remember when we first moved here I thought that living on the waterfront would provide great opportunities to have a swim before breakfast in the summer. I have now lived here for 60 years and have yet to enjoy that pleasure. However I have enjoyed many great swims during other parts of the day during the summer months, and even some late night dips, when we could see the phosphorescence sparkling in the water.

The Moshulu

Esquimalt Harbour had a summer-long visitor in 1935 when the barque *Moshulu* was here having a new suit of sails made in Esquimalt before entering the last grain race between Great Britain and Australia and back. She was built in Port Glasgow, Scotland, in 1904 and was the largest steel-hulled barque ever built. At 3,116 tons she had a length of 335 feet with a beam of 47 feet. Her four masts were 165 feet high and her lower yards were 96 feet long. She had 1,230 steel blocks and the rigging, which was nearly all steel wire line, measured 21 miles. Her 35 sails covered an area of 42,000 square feet. Leaving Esquimalt late in the summer of 1935 the Moshulu sailed to Great Britain, entered and won the last grain race in 91 days return. On her return trip to Great Britain she carried 5,000 tons of grain. (Michael Pope collection)

During the summer of 1934 or '35 the waterfront residents of View Royal were honoured when Emily Carr had her caravan towed out from Victoria and established it at the foot of Beaumont Avenue to do some painting. Some of us teenagers considered her rather an eccentric person, with her monkey and dog. Little did we realize what a famous artist she was.

In the early 30s View Royal roads were nearly all gravel, except the Island Highway. Ladies going into town had trouble keeping their shoes clean on account of dust in the summer and mud in the winter. In order to keep neat and tidy they would walk up to the highway in their gardening shoes and change to a good pair they kept in a mailbox before catching the Veterans Stage into town. At that time of rural mail delivery our mailboxes were at various points along the highway.

Subdivision of part of Sections 8 and 27 of Esquimalt District was completed in 1912. This included the area bounded by the Highway, still shown as Sooke Road, and Esquimalt Harbour, taking in part of Seaview Farm.

Among the early purchasers were Mrs. Riley, Mrs. Bogart, Mr. and Mrs. Sheard and Mr. and Mrs. Cosh, who all built homes in the 1920s. When Mrs. Riley built her house she had to pay for a water line brought down from the main line along the Old Island Highway. When a line was eventually laid along Kerwood everyone who built there had to pay Mrs. Riley $15 to reimburse her for the original cost of her line. The final payment was made in 1946. These homes are still standing, much enlarged and modernized, but none of the original owners is still alive.

Street Names

Some of the original street names, honouring officers of the Royal Navy, have been changed because there were already streets by those names in other parts of Victoria. Seymour Street is now Kerwood, Beresford Avenue is now Bessborough Avenue and Denman Avenue was changed to Kitchener Avenue. These changes were made by notice in the B.C. Gazette in 1939.

However my father felt that this would be a good opportunity to give some recognition to the Stewart family which had farmed the area for so many years and was part of the history of View Royal. He convinced the authorities that the name should be changed from Denman to Stewart Avenue rather than to Kitchener.

Like most teenagers I dreamed of owning my own car. My dreams were fulfilled when I became the proud owner of a 1923 Model T Ford which I bought for the large sum of $15. I was working at the time at Rockhome Gardens, a nursery and landscaping firm on North Quadra Street operated by landscape architects John Hutchison, father of renowned newspaperman Bruce Hutchison, and Norman Rant. Naturally I was very proud of my car which had originally been a touring car but had the back seat cut off and the car made into a small pickup.

My employers knew a good thing when they saw it. They didn't have a delivery vehicle for nursery stock, so it became one of my jobs to use my pride and joy to make deliveries. This was fine until they decided that my car could also be used to pick up chicken manure from a nearby farm. I spent quite a bit of time cleaning that car.

My Model T served well for a couple of years before I sold it at a loss. I only got $11 for it. My next car was an Essex coupe with a rumble seat; I knew I had arrived when I got that. I even let a friend drive the car so I could ride in the rumble seat with my girl friend. It was a tossup which was more fun, driving or riding.

Having spent all my working years dealing with horticulture and landscaping I know that if a tree has been in one spot for 60 years it has developed a pretty substantial root system and it would be very difficult to move. Having lived on Kerwood Avenue in View Royal for 60 years, except for a four-year stint in the RCAF during World War II, I feel that my roots are fairly well established and it would be a mistake to disturb them.

I love View Royal and I am staying until I am dragged out!

Craigflower School And Other Memories

George MacFarlane

Our family lived at 145 Island Highway at the bottom of the Four Mile Hill. Originally the property, which was purchased from the Hudson's Bay Company, consisted of 11 acres and was on the market for $800. My mother procrastinated and, by the time she was won over they had cut it up into three pieces and wanted $400 for each piece, so we bought the middle piece. Later my father bought the neighbouring property when the Charlie Piggott family left, so eventually we had seven acres. Further up towards Craigflower were the Pilgrims, who moved there from Stewart Avenue. Their son Craig was quite a chicken expert and taught me a lot about raising chickens, and I had quite a little chicken operation myself while I was going to school. Next to them was Sam Bell who, along with his wife, raised race horses and was well known in the racing circuit.

I remember the daily coach from Hatley Park. Every morning about 10 o'clock it would go by, drawn by two beautiful black horses on its way into Victoria. The uniformed driver picked up the mail and supplies and returned about mid-afternoon five days a week without fail, in all weathers. [James Dunsmuir's widow lived in the baronial mansion at Hatley Park until her death in 1937.]

Beside the railway track along Deadman's Creek was a large pond which had

been created when the railway trestle was filled in. We called it the bullrush pond because of the bullrushes which grew around the edge, and it froze in the winter to give us an excellent skating area. It was nearly always in shade so the ice stayed for a long time. The area has been filled in and is now part of the playing field of the school built in 1951.

I attended the second Craigflower School across the road from the original 1855 school. It had four classrooms and four teachers, two classes to each room. Miss Styan taught Grades 1 and 2, Miss Scholfield 3 and 4, Miss Foster 5 and 6, and George Taylor, the principal, taught 7 and 8. We were happy children and

The second Craigflower School opened in 1912 across the road from the 1855 school. Side view shows Grade 7 and 8 classrooms. (Victoria School Board Archives)

I think it was quite a good school, although we were limited on the amount of sports we took part in because of the lack of staff.

But I particularly remember the janitor, a delightful elderly lady whose name I think was Miss Richardson, red-headed, hair greying. She said that her family arrived on the barque Tory and they were part of the early Hudson's Bay farm at Colwood. She seemed like a second mother to the children at school. Besides tending the furnace and doing janitor work she helped look after us and bandage scraped knees and that sort of thing.

I remember two items that seem to have disappeared when the school was demolished, and I wish I knew what happened to them. One was a beautiful B.C. coat of arms done in tile on the floor on the front entrance facing Admirals Road. We weren't allowed to use that entrance because George Taylor said we would probably scratch the tile and it shouldn't be defaced, it was such a beautiful work of art. Everyone, including parents, teachers and pupils, used the back entrance.

The other was a large old British cannon which used to sit near the front entrance. After the second World War I drove by and noticed it had been moved down the embankment to the lower lawn which was never used for sports, although it would have made a suitable tennis court. A few years later I noticed the cannon was missing. I hope it's in safe hands.

While I was at school Craigflower bridge was rebuilt. It was out for some time and there was no means of getting across the Gorge. So old Mr. Brookman, who arrived in the area about 1930-31 and had Brookman's store on the corner of Admirals and Gorge roads, ferried passengers across the Gorge neck in his boat so they could get on the bus and travel into Victoria. Those of us who couldn't afford the fare for Brookman would sneak past the watchman and travel on the beams of the decking of the new bridge. In hindsight this was probably rather dangerous, but at the time it was challenging and we kids thought we were quite clever to be able to go back and forth and dodge the watchman.

The land behind the school and all the land we now call Christie Point, probably 100 acres, including the Craigflower farmhouse, and the barns across the Island Highway where the Craigflower Motel is, were leased by H. E. Newton. Mr. Newton posted No Trespassing signs and designated the whole area a bird sanctuary. He must have been a man of means. He presented copies of the federal Department of Mines 1928 publication "Birds of Western Canada" by P. A. Traverner to students who showed proficiency in what was then called nature study.

Across Portage Inlet from Mr. Newton's was Deadman's River. Going up the river on the right hand side near the intersection of Helmcken Road was E. W. Tribe's dairy. Tribe was known as Commander Tribe because he was the commanding officer of the Rainbow Sea Cadets, a fine gentleman and very dedicated. He recruited most of the boys in View Royal into the Sea Cadet Corps. These included myself, Eric Fisher, Richard Fetherstonhaugh, Roger Mann, Albert Pegg, Ernie Foster and others. He had a Model A Ford which he used to deliver milk and to transport the lot of us to Sea Cadet headquarters at Rithet's pier. In the summer we would ride our bicycles to town. All of us share very fond memories of Commander Tribe who did an excellent job for the young boys of the district.

Nearby were two fox farms. One on the river was owned by Mr. D. W. Hanbury, and one between the river and the Old Island Highway was Mr. Hanson's Ideal Fox Farm. I had dealings with Mr. Hanson, a man of Scandinavian background and no sense of humour. One day one of his foxes escaped and came down the Four Mile Hill to our property. Much to my horror it got into my chicken yard, grabbed a chicken and took off. In those days shooting wild animals was in vogue. My father always left the .22 at home and told me to use it to protect the birds and the fowl and the game and so on, so I shot the fox. I suspected it was Mr. Hanson's because I'd missed one or two chickens before and I assumed the same fox had taken them. So I bundled it up on my bicycle and took the corpse to him. He was furious. He said I should have told him what happened and he would have come up and caught the valuable fox. We had quite an argument. He got the dead fox and I got 50 cents for one chicken.

I had a special cedar dugout canoe made by Harold Baird of Port Renfrew whom I met when I used to travel up the west coast on the tugboats with my father. It was a small, lightweight canoe, about seven feet long, beautifully built and fitted out for rowing. I first kept it at the bottom of the Four Mile Hill in the bushes on Mr. Newton's property, illegally. But the long and tedious journey out over the mud flats at low tide persuaded me to move it over to Thetis Cove in Esquimalt Harbour to the float of an old gentleman we knew as the crab fisherman. I could get there from our property by walking along the railway tracks. The kind gentleman looked after my canoe, and covered it with burlap sacking on hot days to prevent it from cracking in the sun.

Close by was the CPR wharf and small tank farm. At the wharf in those days the CPR had two ships laid up. One was a freighter which had been fitted with large tanks for the pilchard oil trade until this disappeared. On the other side of the wharf was the old SS Patricia, a long, thin high-speed vessel in her day, probably capable of 30 knots.

Next was the old Tod cannery, serviced by a tender named Olive M bringing scows of fish from Sooke fish traps in daily for processing in the cannery. The Olive M is still about, I saw her on Pender Island two years ago. The superintendent of the cannery was a Mr. Rassmussen.

Along the waterfront towards Dyke Point was White Lady Beach. It was a favorite spot for picnicking. People from Victoria would come to swim as well as

View Royal folks. There were open areas where we could play ball and have a family gathering. It was very popular until about World War II when Captain W. B. L. Holms bought the property and fenced it off and that was the end of that.

Among the families I remember well were Frank and Honor Mann and their sons Christopher and Roger. Frank Mann swam every day of the year down off the beach below their home at 267 View Royal Avenue. Even when the water was bitterly cold he would have his dip in the water and rush back up to his shower. He owned a number of bakeries in Victoria, Molly's Bakery and the Pie Shop among others.

Another family I remember well, and lost track of much to my sorrow, were the Pooleys, a California family who lived in the large home on Bessborough Road built by Doctor Holden. I used to visit the twin sons who went to Craigflower School. The senior Mrs. Pooley, Grandma Pooley, was in residence and looked after the boys. Their father was head of Majestic Radio in the United States and I believe divorced. At any rate he had a number of lady friends who would visit from time to time for short periods and when he was visiting the boys would say don't come round to the house, Dad's home. But when he'd leave they'd always want me around and we'd play on the

Dr. Donald Holden built one of View Royal's large homes in 1920 on a point at the foot of Bessborough Road. It was later bought by the Goldring family and has since had a succession of owners. The gardens which were open for church functions have disappeared under a strata development.(Robert Duffus photo)

rather extensive property and also on their floats and wharves. I think Mr. Pooley sold the property to another American. The Pooleys disappeared and I have never heard of them since.

I also visited Chantecler out on the highway, as a friend of one of the sons. Harold Alexander and his family, a negro family, had a thriving business which in those days I guess we referred to as bootlegging. However it was well done and acceptable to the community. No one complained about it.

Old Mr. Keys had a large garden of bamboo at his place on the Old Island Highway across from Lumley's grocery store. He was a great authority on the subject and it was a real pleasure to visit and have him lecture on different kinds of bamboo, where they were from and how they were propagated.

Lastly I recall one other gentleman who lived next to the Four Mile House. If I remember correctly he was Mr. Nalley who made salad dressing in a little garage which he converted into a small factory and I presume it was the start of the famous Nalley's salad dressing.

Jiggs And The Minifie Goats

Maureen Duffus

When I was three or four Grandfather Morrison used to take me with him when he walked to Miss Stewart's cowbarn for milk. We went down the hill from 265 View Royal Avenue to the rocks where the road runs into Beaumont and jogs right. On these rocks were Mrs. Minifie's goats, and guarding the goats was Mrs. Minifie's dog Jiggs. Large, black and wolf-like, he was a frightening sight but Grandfather would wave his walking stick at the dog and we would progress unmolested. Mrs. Minifie and others said Jiggs was a gentle dog but I never believed them. Mrs. Plowright had goats, too, but these were safely behind a fence. Goat's milk was the thing in the early 30s - it was the health food equivalent of today's two per cent yogurt or oat bran or whatever.

When we reached the barn Miss Stewart and Mr. Colclough, who helped on the farm, would offer a cup of milk 'fresh from the cow.' Not my idea of a treat, I can tell you. I thought it tasted like the cow-smells in the barn.

My father, R. S. Stuart Yates, built our cabin below my grandparents' house. It was on a ledge above the shore, so I spent my first years listening to the waves at night and the foghorn in the morning, lovely soothing sounds. I think I learned to count seconds, watching the Fisgard lighthouse beam through the bedroom window at night.

Playing on the beach was great, climbing the rocks at either side of the little bay, fishing for minnows, poking sea anenomes until they closed their little fringes. One year there was a single swan, bigger than I was, who came begging. A bad-tempered bird, it bit the hand that fed it. Pet seagulls were safe though. You think gulls are all the same? Consider Tilly and Silly. They flew in together for regular handouts, Tilly the boss in proper gull-grey and white, Silly a messy mottled brownish follower. They established exclusive landing rights on our part of the beach at feeding time for at least two years.

Before I learned to swim I used to drift around in a rubber tire. One day the waves took me to the Plowright side of the bay, all of 50 feet away for goodness sake, and I made a fuss. Then it was off to the the Crystal Garden and Archie McKinnon for swimming lessons.

When my sisters and I were older we caught large crabs off the rocks by poking sticks into their claws, hauling them up and carrying them by their two back legs to a pot of seawater boiling on a beach fire. We knew they didn't really cry out, but air bubbling up certainly sounded like a crab in pain. We overcame our animal-rights scruples easily.

Digging clams at low tide, gathering bark and driftwood to store in the sheds behind the wharf for the fireplaces, were other pastimes of waterfront children.

Older boys sometimes caught rock cod off the point, and some years large schools of smelts came right into shore. We stood on the shore with nets to scoop them into buckets. I don't remember liking to eat them but they were probably considered a treat. Mr. Deacon, ace fisherman who lived in the cottage below Plowright's house, caught proper fish in the harbour all year round. I went fishing with him once and we caught a pregnant dogfish.

Neighbours were the Plowrights and the Manns. Next was Dr. John Watson, a music teacher. My parents, surprised their four-year-old could pick out a tune on grandmother's piano, sent me for a lesson. I thought the limit of piano playing was hitting the same notes with the left hand at the same time as the right. Poor distinguished Dr. Watson. I think he tried to explain but his idea of making music didn't interest me. End of lessons. Across the road was Miss Hosie's house, perched high on the rocks.

Older still: rowing over to Magazine Island, which we didn't know was really called Cole Island, and to the islands across the harbour - more goats. Then all the way to Fisgard lighthouse, a forbidden adventure because the inside was abandoned and rotting - and spooky.

We used to climb the rocks to White Lady Point for secret meetings on the beach around the other side, until Captain Holms built his house and Mrs. Holms shooed us away, unfairly we thought. We were there first. Well, second. The Indians whom we heard digging clams or holding ceremonies across the water were really first.

My sister Beverly and I went to school at Craigflower when we spent winters at the enlarged cottage during the Depression. (We thought we were staying there as a special treat, not knowing until years later that our Oak Bay house had to be rented because father's clients couldn't pay their bills.)

After the family moved back to Oak Bay we still spent summers at the cottage and had beach parties on our birthdays. Everyone was impressed with the Japanese lanterns father hung all along the path that wound down to the beach. Next to the cottage was a cabin overhanging a steep unstable bank. It served as a guest house, changing place and rainy-day playhouse. It was not well built. One rainy night years later when my husband and I were staying in the cottage we heard the 'annex' take a prolonged and dramatic tumble down the soggy bank.

We lived in the cottage for a year or so after we came back to Victoria in the mid-1950s. Mrs. Plowright was still there in her unfinished house up the hill, but View Royal was changing even then. Modest cottages and bungalows were sprouting additions and becoming grander, and mother eventually decided, reluctantly, to sell the place.

My husband and I moved back to View Royal in 1961, to a small farm on Atkins Road. Our two sons grew up there, climbing trees, holding secret meetings in tree forts and old sheep sheds, and exploring the harbour in kayaks, canoes and rowboats as I had done 30 years before.

Sawing Logs and Building Rafts

Milton Williams

My grandparents, Malcolm and Lydia Morrison, and their seven children came from Pictou, Nova Scotia, where grandfather had a ship chandlery, around the turn of the century. In the early 20s they lived with my aunt Ethel Morrison who bought the property at 265 View Royal Avenue when she returned from overseas nursing duty.

During the summers the house was crowded when my mother brought my sister Gwen and myself over from Vancouver. Later my Aunt Alice and her husband stayed there too until Uncle Bob built a cabin down near the beach. Aunt Ethel, who was school nurse at Lampson Street School, moved out each summer

Gwen and Milton Williams with a young cousin on one of Milton's rafts. In the background a flag flies above the Plowrights' teahouse on the rocks near White Lady Point. (Morrison album)

when she went back on active duty in the army, nursing at Fort Rodd Hill or Work Point barracks.

There were quite a few young people in the neighbourhood then. Charlie Plowright, Pat Colclough and Gordon Fawcett were friends, and Gwen's girl friends included Margaret Fawcett and Phyllis Riley.

Magazine Island was still occupied, with a caretaker living on the site. We used to hear a little one-cylinder boat putt-putting over every day on inspection. We were told it was a seized rum-runner.

One year during the depression my father was helping Wilf Gouge with major repairs to the old Four Mile House when they found a cache of bottles of whisky hidden between the walls. No doubt they had been there since 1920 or so when Canadian prohibition ended.

I used to help grandfather saw piles of driftwood to store in the sheds behind the wharf. When it got to be too much for grandfather to carry it up the steep path to the house Mr. Colclough rigged up a rope and pulley system to haul it up the bank. Raft building was another summer activity, with grandfather supervising the selection of logs and how to nail driftwood planks. These masterpieces of marine construction never survived the winter storms

Three Clever English Ladies

Mrs. Frances Minifie, Mrs. Alice Colclough and Mrs. Doris Robinson were three English ladies who found their way to View Royal between 1929 and 1939. They lived within a few blocks of each other and are remembered as 'eccentric but brilliant' by children who enjoyed visiting them.

Mrs. Minifie, mother of well-known Canadian writer and broadcaster James M. Minifie, came first, by way of Vanquard, Saskatchewan. For reasons no one remembers she left Saskatchewan on her own in 1929 and, with help from a sister, built a house on Beaumont Avenue. She either brought or bought a piano, for she was a classically trained pianist, and gave mu-

sic lessons to a few neighbourhood children. Most knew her for her goats, and the dog cart she filled with fire wood gathered from the beaches.

In 1931 Frances Minifie broke a leg, either falling off a horse she used to ride into town or falling on the rocks while gathering wood. (Both stories are told with certainty, but the horse version is less convincing.) In this incapacitated condition she wrote to her friends Lawrence and Mary Fieldhouse in Saskatchewan and persuaded them to come to Victoria to look after her. Their son George remembers helping Mrs. Minifie haul wood up to the house. He also recalls she tried to teach him piano.

View Royal Avenue, ca 1930, a dirt track to Beaumont and the Minifie house, fenced fields of the Stewart farm on either side. The Stewart cowbarn was close to the fence on the right. (Minifie album)

Frances Minifie with dog, goats and wood cart, as children of the 30s remember her. The old Tod cannery in the background suggests the photo was taken near Dyke Point. (Minifie album)

Mrs. Minifie and her broadcaster son James, a well known war correspondent in the Spanish Civil War and World War II, and later Washington correspondent for the Canadian Broadcasting Corporation, in her View Royal garden. (Minifie album)

Mrs. Colclough and her husband came from Pine Lake, Alberta, at about the same time and bought the house next to Mrs. Minifie, on the corner of Beaumont and View Royal Avenue. Alice Colclough was known as the local intellectual who read a lot and wrote for newspapers and magazines. Beth MacLean remembers that Mrs. Colclough had books for children to read and arranged for a subscription to the children's magazine Wee Wisdom. This led to Beth's first published work, a poem in Wee Wisdom.

The third lady was Beth's mother, Doris Robinson, another classically trained pianist who first came to Canada to teach at the exclusive Queen Margaret's School for girls in Duncan. When Mrs. Robinson and her three children came to live on Pallisier Road they had no money for a piano so Mrs. Minifie invited the former concert pianist to play at her house any time.

George Fieldhouse remembers some eccentricities, like the chickens hanging in Mrs. Minifie's stairwell by their necks. They were ready to cook, according to Mrs. Minifie, when they dropped to the floor. George says she was a terrible cook. Her treats for the boys who helped bring in the wood were so inedible they were tossed into the woods as soon as the boys were out of sight of the house.

But the three English ladies, surrounded by goats and cows and chickens, kept up with their music and writing. Mrs. Robinson's daughter Beth, who loved visiting Mrs. Colclough, remembers her mother admitting that her friends were a bit eccentric, but always added "we're fortunate to know them, they are so rich with knowledge."

Lavender Cottage, at the corner of Beaumont and View Royal Avenue, was home to Mr. and Mrs. Dudley Colclough and their son Pat in the 1930s. It is one of the few View Royal houses that has not changed since it was built by music teacher Dr. Watson in the 1920s. (Gladys Durrant drawing)

Queenie At The Plough

(Compiled from several interviews)

One of the delights of life for View Royal children was a ride in the cow-drawn cart pulled by Queenie, a Jersey-Guernsey cross bred who lived a pampered life in a log cabin with her daughter Daisy on the five-acre farm of Mr. and Mrs. William Duval, near the top of the Four Mile Hill.

The Duvals moved to View Royal in 1930. The farm was too small to keep a horse employed year-round, so Mr. Duval trained his cows to do the ploughing. He used a regular harness with a padded collar adapted to the way cows (or, in earlier days, oxen) pull from the top of the neck. Training the cows took patience and months of work until they were used to the harness and responded to commands. Daisy learned by working in harness with her mother.

Queenie's chores included hauling loads of manure for the alfalfa crop, bringing in wood for the winter, cultivating between rows of raspberries, boysenberries and currants, and ploughing. Her workday was short, never more than two hours at a time, and the remarkable Queenie continued to yield a good supply of milk for many years.

The Duvals also raised as many as 300 rabbits at a time for market, and calves from a few days old. A small flock of chickens, a watchdog and a Persian cat were added to the animal population at various times.

George MacFarlane Remembers:

I remember Bill Duval who lived up on the top of the Four Mile Hill, near Lumley's grocery store. Bill was an expert gardener who made a living growing and selling vegetables but he used his milk cows to pull the plough. He swore it didn't hurt the cows, but we thought it was quite unusual. He and Mrs. Duval, who lost their own son in a drowning accident in Shawnigan Lake some years previously, were kind friends to the children of the neighbourhood.

Village Grove townhouses behind the firehall are part of the old Duval farm.

Bill Duval's versatile cow Queenie taking Brian and Elizabeth Pearce for a ride, early 1950s. (McTavish collection)

Christmas At Quandalla

Phyllis McAdams

Auntie Wood, as the late Mrs. J. F. O. Wood was usually called, had been known for her special way with dogs and cats since 1924 when she and her late husband started training show dogs and breeding wire-haired terriers and Scotties. The first Quandalla sign went up in 1928 in Victoria, and in 1930 the Woods were breeding German shepherds and cocker spaniels at their home at the corner of the Old Island Highway and Plowright Road.

At first they had no thought of boarding animals but they were persuaded to by people impressed with their method of caring for dogs. To accommodate the growing list of boarders they moved to 21 Atkins Road in 1951. The kennels had guest houses with awnings and separate runways set in a charming garden surrounded by green painted fences.

Mrs. Wood of Quandalla Kennels

The animals were Auntie Wood's family. Some stayed for many months like Kiltie Cameron, a Scottie, who came for three months every winter for 14 years. Willie, a dachshund from Ottawa, always bustled to his usual compartment with an "Auntie Wood, I'm home" air about him. They came from as far away as Africa. Animals arriving by plane were met personally by Mrs. Wood, who shipped animals in her care to Switzerland, Germany, England and South Africa, as well as all over North America.

When I did a story in a local paper about Mrs. Wood one Christmas, dog and cat guests were checking in for the holiday season. Arriving by car, boat and plane, they were welcomed by Auntie Wood, who personally saw they were comfortably settled in their respective compartments. That Christmas Popsy, Fritty, Crumpet and a Siamese called Sena (he was on an extended visit while his owners were in England) each found a red felt toy mouse in their quarters at the Pussy Cat Motel.

Dog guests were housed in the main Quandalla kennels. In contrast to the quiet, sedate Pussy Cat Motel there was some boisterous chatter and exuberant playfulness there, but one kind, though commanding, word from Auntie Wood reminded her guests rowdiness could not be tolerated. That Christmas Punchy, an American spaniel, had five lively puppies to add to the jollity of the season while Rastus, a kindly coal black German shepherd owned by Auntie Wood, kept a watchful vigil over Quandalla.

It was Mrs. Wood's wish that when she died the kennels would be closed. There are no boarders now.

Friends And Adventures

Jim Wilmshurst

In 1922 my mother, father, two brothers and I lived across from Palmer Station near the Island Meat Packers. My father worked for Patrick Burns, who owned the plant for 24 years. It was built close to the E.&N. railway and trains would bring live chickens, turkeys and geese from Alberta. One of our jobs was to catch these birds, crate them up and send them down to Store Street in Victoria.

Palmer Station was named for the Palmer family of the well-known Huntley and Palmer Biscuit Company family. Their house on a high rock overlooking Esquimalt Harbour was called Gibraltar. They had lived there since just after World War I. Mrs. Palmer kindly let us children go through her property to go swimming. She was one of my first customers when I opened the Betty Ann Bakery in 1947. She was very generous and used to make donations of baked goods from my store to the Old Age Pensioners hall in Victoria. I never met Mr. Palmer as he was ill and confined to the house.

I remember two gentlemen who lived across from where Louie's Market is today. Frank White and Frank Cox had a job of felling trees between the E.&N. and the CNR tracks. They cut the trees into cordwood and stacked it into piles and sold it to make a living. I also remember Mr. Lambert, a bachelor who lived next to Mrs. Palmer's driveway. He owned property at Lakehill at Borden Street and I used to work for him haying during the summer holidays.

Another summer job was working for Mr. and Mrs. Creed who had a chicken farm in the vicinity of Creed Road. I had to clean out each of the buildings and sort eggs. Their son operated Creed's Nursery on Shelbourne Street.

Across the street from the Creeds lived long-time residents Dr. H. A. Francis and his daughter Phyllis. I remember one day Dr. Francis came to my parents with a petition asking people to sign if they were in favour of having a school built at the corner of Helmcken Road and the Island highway where I later had the bakery.

The Barker family were also early residents. I went to the second Craigflower School with Kay, who is now Mrs. McConnan, and her brother Dick. Mr. Barker looked after the Todds' summer home between Thetis Lake and Pike Lake, so the children had quite a way to go to school. They rode their bikes to Atkins Road, then either walked to school or, later, caught the school 'bus' - a small red Ford van.

Palmer Station, 1993. (Michael Pope photo)

When we were going to school Dr. Holden used to drive us in his car. Another person I went to school with was Alice Heron. Her family lived on View Royal Avenue at Bessborough. We were allowed to go through their property to swim in Limekiln Cove.

Joe Bailey, a lightweight boxing champion, made the Four Mile House his headquarters. He taught Tommy Fielding the art of boxing in a small shack next to the Colwood beer parlour.

At this time, 1923-24, the Fulton family had a small store at the corner of Admirals and Craigflower Road. The first store in View Royal was operated by Miss Pimlott at the top of the Four Mile Hill. We kids thought this was great as we could now buy penny candies after school. (Shirley Pilgrim Wade remembers the candies on the many days Miss Pimlott forgot to pull the window blinds down. The results were sold at discount prices to the children and were known as 'melted wellies." Mr. Lumley took over the grocery just before the war then leased it to Bert Thomas. Bill and Frances Barrett took over in 1947 and built living quarters above the store.

The big house on Mr. Plasterer's Fort Victoria property was originally built as a roadhouse called Chante-cler by the Alexander family. The Fisher family ran a small store next to where Louie's Market is now, along with gas pumps operated by Len and Cyril Parsons.

On Helmcken Road by the railway trestle below the school a woman had two Airedale dogs and a small cart. Once or twice a week she drove into Victoria with them. We were always told to be careful with those dogs when we were kids.

Phyllis McAdams wrote a story about the bakery in 1965: Jim Wilmshurst was a craftsman at his trade. From 1929 to 1947 he worked at a bakery in Victoria. When he opened the Betty Ann Bakery in December, 1947, all the baking was done at the back of the shop. Jim's day started at 5 a.m. Bread, rolls, butterhorns, Danish pastries and doughnuts were made first. Next came the cakes, fruit and meat pies, tarts and cookies. The brick-shelved oven held 200 loaves. A long-handled paddle 'peeled' the oven, that is it was used to remove the baked goods. Weekdays there were two bakings, and four at weekends. Closing of the Betty Ann Bakery was a sad loss for View Royal. The luscious baked goods and aroma of fresh-baked bread were gone forever.

REPLICA OF
FORT VICTORIA BUILDING

G. DURRANT '93

Dr. Herbert Plasterer built this replica of a Fort Victoria building using the same construction methods employed by the French Canadians who built the original. (Gladys Durrant drawing)

West Burnside Families

Richard Rant

I was born in View Royal in 1921. My grandfather, who had been a captain in the Bengal Lancers, came to B.C. around the turn of the century and was a gold commissioner at Atlin in northern B.C. He had a house on Burnside Road about where the storage sheds are, at the intersection with the Trans Canada Highway and the Old Island Highway. My parents' house was on Thetis Lake Road, which used to run right through to the old highway before the new one was built. That house was torn down and I was born in the second house near the present Marler Road in the Edgelow subdivision. North of this were the Grants and the Heron family who had a house across Deadman's Creek.

There were two Chinese vegetable gardens, one between Chilco Road and Thetis Lake Road, and another off Burnside Road across from Creed Road, probably leased from Dr. Francis. Captain Lund had the farm at the end of Chilco Road.

My playground, and later my paper routes, ranged from Thetis Lake to Parson's Bridge and through the fields across Burnside to homes of friends who lived near Helmcken Road.

We used to swim at Thetis Lake even before the old watershed was opened to the public. The caretaker, Mr. Massey, lived in a small house opposite the present entrance and didn't stop us from going to the lake. At first it was just a few of us who lived west of Helmcken Road - the Wilmshurts, Fishers and Rants. After the View Royal boys found out about it there was quite a large group of us. One day we went to the little bay to the left as you approach the lake and found a dead man, a suicide, under a tree. Two of the older boys went off to tell Mr. Massey, but he wasn't

The impressive house on the Old Island Highway at Burnett Road was a roadhouse run by the Alexander family in the 1930s. Later owners were Mr. and Mrs. Morrow who built auto court bungalows in matching architectural style. (Gladys Durrant drawing)

there so they had to run all the way to Miss Pimlott's store at the top of the Four Mile Hill before they got to a phone to call the police.

We all went to Craigflower School. I remember one of the teachers was strict about checking to see if our hands were clean. I always had to do farm chores in the mornings before school but she made no allowance for this if there was any dirt under my fingernails.

We knew Mrs. Palmer of 'Gibraltar' who was very well off but so good to kids. Once she gave me a silver dollar which seemed like a fortune in Depression days. I used to deliver the paper to Mr. Goldring who lived in the big house at the end of Bessborough Road.

We all knew the Alexanders at Chantecler, who ran a very careful 'roadhouse' as it was politely called. Later the Morrows bought it and ran it as a motor court. The Price family still had the Six Mile House.

My father, Gordon Rant, was a general contractor and my uncle Norman had a nursery, Rockholme Gardens. Later, because of the Depression we moved to Bralorne, B.C., where my father had a job at the mines. He was a captain in World War II.

After driving tanks for five years during the war I came back to View Royal and lived on Suzanne Place which was part of the land Fats Atkinson cleared for his subdivision. We moved to the Highland District in 1961.

The Fenns Of Fenton Road

Phyllis McAdams

A very short dead-end road tucked away off View Royal Avenue across from the Four Mile House had a name change around 1965. Many years before the road existed the area was parkland belonging to Mr. and Mrs. Peter Calvert who built the Four Mile House and ran it as an inn. Their daughter Mary, later Mrs. Wilfred Gouge, pastured horses and cows in the meadowland abundant with wild flowers.

When the area was later subdivided it was known as the Collingwood Estate, with lots selling for $50 each. Sometime around 1930 Mr. Bernard Fenn, an English lawyer, and his wife, an artist, bought property there.

They lived in a tent, even in the coldest winter months, until their house was finished. Oldtimers recall their tent lighted by lamp and candles, glowing in the snow.

They survived the hardships of 'roughing it' and named a lane that ran by their house Fenn Road. When Mrs. Fenn died her husband moved to Cadboro Bay and a road there was named Fenn Road. This led to confusion and annoyance, especially when gravel and lumber trucks with grinding brakes discovered they had reached the wrong Fenn Road. The miniature road is now called Fenton Road.

Ship's Cabin On The Rocks

Phyllis McAdams

It was May, 1948, in a downpour of rain, when my husband Wallie and I first took up residence in View Royal. We bought property with a cabin on it, and would live in the cabin until we built a new home. We would do the building ourselves in our spare time.

The cabin was unique. It was the upper structure off a ship that had been dismantled at Victoria Machinery Depot. Mr. and Mrs. Harry Waring had it hauled to the View Royal property and transformed the interior into a livable home with a kitchen and dining area, small bedroom, bathroom with shower, and a tiny hallway. On the kitchen side were two doors that would have opened onto the deck of the ship, whose name they could not recall.

The unusual little home had a flat roof and windows all around. We planned to build around the ship's cabin, put a roof over all, then tear out the cabin. Friends organized a work bee and the cement foundation was poured in a day. Our work tools were a hammer, handsaw, level, elbow grease and muscle power. We hauled lumber on a trailer back of the car as our finances allowed. Work progressed slowly during that rainy, blustery summer. When winter came one thickness of the cabin walls did not keep out the freezing cold. Water pipes froze and burst. We bundled up in longjohns, pants and layers of sweaters. To sit on a hot water bottle with my feet in the oven was sheer joy.

Our stove was a wood burner. The stovepipe jutted out of the wall, pointing heavenward, sporting a tin coolie hat.I often complained "It looks too frail for the important job it has to do." One windy day I saw the worrisome thing at the kitchen window doing a macabre dance at the end of a wire. Frantic, I climbed a ladder and with ten thumbs wired it back in place.

By the following winter our unfinished kitchen and dinette were usable and warm. Our new sitting room was ready for the fireplace and chimney which was to be built on an outside wall. It was late December and the weather was mild. We hired a bricklayer. Christmas morning we were happy with good old Christmas cheer and goodwill to the world - until we realized that overnight the temperature had dropped to a freezing low.

Our chimney was leaning at a rakish angle, the still damp mortar frozen and ruined. With a shove it toppled to the ground. Before it could be rebuilt in the spring every brick had to be scraped clean of mortar. I fell heir to that job.

At last the sun shone after the rain, wind, snow and freezing temperatures had plagued us for so long, and spring was in the air. But I could hear running water. It couldn't be a burst pipe? No. The snow was melting on a high rock formation in the back garden. As the basement had no back or front doors as yet, a river of melting snow was rushing under the house to the street. We dug ditches well into the night.

The time came when the ship's cabin had to be torn down. We did it with regret. But we saved one wall with three of the ship's windows as part of our house - a lasting memory to a ship whose name we will never know.

The View Royal Garage

Len R. Parsons

In the spring of 1939, the premises that my partner and cousin Cyril (Cy) Parsons and I operated as an auto repair garage were sold. This property was at the southwest corner of Helmcken Road and the Island Highway. We decided to build a new outlet in the area but there were several problems. Restrictions imposed by the new Coal and Petroleum Control Board of British Columbia, the ominous war clouds gathering, and the difficulty of finding commercially zoned property were major worries. The only possible location was on the south side of the Old Island Highway between Beaumont Avenue and Plowright Road.

Our application to the Fuel Control Board for a permit and license to sell fuel products was finally granted after considerable discussion and red tape delays. Contractors, building materials and station equipment were almost impossible to obtain due to the imminence of war. M. P. Paine Contractors agreed to undertake construction, but could find no firm available to clear, excavate and level the sloped and undulating land. However, Don Ross did the job alone with his team of horses and a steel scoop. He did a terrific job, felling trees, clearing heavy undergrowth, and moving tons of clay dirt. Rapid construction followed during

The first fire truck, Cy Parson's car with A.R.P. pump, at Parsons' garage. (Pope collection)

The familiar little green and white Texaco garage was one of the last independent service stations in Victoria. (Parsons album)

which time the Fairbanks Morse Co. of Victoria scoured the Island for equipment. By midsummer we were operational. Two months later, World War II began, bringing with it fuel rationing and great difficulties trying to find replacement car and truck parts.

The View Royal A.R.P. was formed with primitive equipment consisting mainly of a truck converted for fire duty, with hand water tanks and pumps. A Bickle Seagrave pressure pump with engine was mounted on a two-wheel trailer to tow behind the truck. A 300-gallon wood stave vat was erected at the rear of our property to provide a head of water for fire use.

The View Royal Garage served the area for 46 years, finally closing its doors in 1981.

The Louie Family

(From an interview with Poy Yee Louie)

Everyone in View Royal knows Louie's store, and many remember the older Mr. Louie who used to deliver vegetables to the door in a truck. But hardly anyone knows the story behind this pioneer Vancouver Island family that built up the mini-supermarket at 387 Island Highway from a tiny grocery on the site of an old livery stable.

The story begins in the early 1900s when Loong Jai Louie, grandfather of the present owners, left Canton for North America. He came to San Francisco, then to Vancouver Island where he worked in a sawmill at Ladysmith, and stayed there for the rest of his life. In 1920 he brought his 17-year-old son, Hoy Louie, the late Mr. Louie who was so well known in View Royal, to join him. Hoy worked with his father and saved his wages so he could return to China to marry Poy Yee in 1922. Hoy came back alone, unable to bring his bride with him, and continued to save and send money to his wife. He made visits every few years but was never able to bring his wife and children back to Canada with him.

In 1937 Hoy was concerned about news of the Japanese invasion of China and their move towards Canton. He wrote to his family and had them travel to the relative safety of Kowloon only a few months ahead of the invasion. Henry Louie, the present owner of Louie's Foods, was born there. It was a difficult time for Mrs. Louie and the children as they waited until the Japanese

were defeated and they were able to go back to their own home in Canton.

There were a few quiet years when Hoy Louie paid several visits, and the oldest daughter, Chi Fong, mar-

Mr. and Mrs. Hoy Louie, shortly after Mrs. Louie was finally allowed to come to Canada in 1951. (Louie family photo)

ried and went to live in Trinidad. New dangers appeared as the Communists took over the country, and once again Hoy Louie arranged to move his family, hoping to bring them to Victoria where he lived on a five-acre farm near the present University of Victoria stadium. He grew vegetables and delivered them door to door with a horse and wagon, a familiar sight in Victoria.

Meanwhile, Mrs. Louie and the children moved to Hong Kong to wait for immigration papers. It was a year-long wait in cramped quarters, and Mrs. Louie was hard-pressed to care for her family. When word finally came in 1950 there was a terrible blow; only the five children, including a 14-month old baby, could leave. The authorities decided their mother's health was too poor.

The children, Bing, Dora, Fay, Henry and baby Carol, left on the Ss. President for San Francisco and travelled by train to B.C. Eighteen-year-old Bing spoke a little English, and Dora, 16, cared for the the baby and the other children. Ten-year-old Henry remembers it as a huge adventure, but he also remembers the sadness and pain of leaving without their mother.

Now, at the age of 86, Poy Yee Louie still can't forget her great apprehension for the children. After an agonizing year she was allowed to come to Canada when immigration officials decided she was well enough. She had simply been suffering from exhaustion. She flew to Victoria in 1951, to the great joy of her family. A daughter, Ida, was born in Victoria and later attended View Royal School.

A son and daughter, Fay and Dora, opened the first Louie's grocery store a few years later with help from their father. The old building is still a landmark but for the past 15 years Henry Louie and his wife Ann have presided over the new larger store next door. Hoy Louie died in 1992, but Poy Yee Louie is still recognized with affection when she appears in the popular grocery known simply as Louie's.

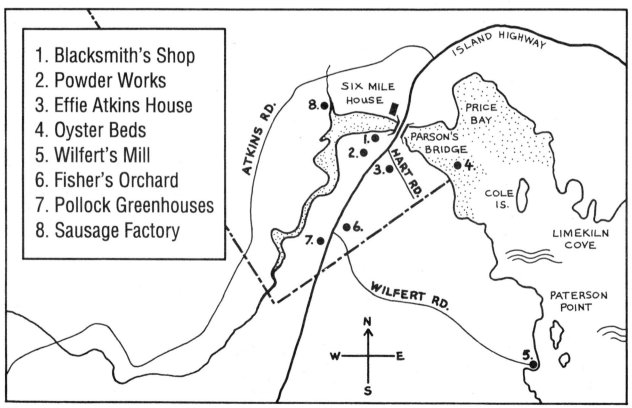

1. Blacksmith's Shop
2. Powder Works
3. Effie Atkins House
4. Oyster Beds
5. Wilfert's Mill
6. Fisher's Orchard
7. Pollock Greenhouses
8. Sausage Factory

West of Parson's Bridge.

The Other Side Of The Bridge

View Royal does not, as many believe, end at Parson's Bridge. It continues up Highway 1A through a commercial strip, along the semi-rural part of Atkins Road which winds between the Esquimalt and Nanaimo Railway tracks and the Galloping Goose trail, and includes the well-hidden waterfront of Hart Road.

Sources for the following information include Earl and David Pollock, Mrs. Jimmy Mabb, Mrs. Dolly McInnes and Dick Rant, who helped piece together the stories of the mills, kilns, brick works, blacksmith shops, auto courts, orchards and farms of earlier years.

At the south end of Parson's bridge, opposite the Six Mile House Hotel, was Will Simpson's house overlooking the water. His blacksmith shop and brass foundry were next, and he had a small mink farm behind the foundry. The buildings stood where an assortment of business premises, once a farmer's market, now await improvement. He also bred canaries and Mrs. Mabb remembers how surprisingly gentle his big blacksmith's hands were when he helped one of his egg-bound canaries.

Next to the foundry was a powder magazine, originally Hamilton Powder Works, later owned by Canadian Industries Limited (C.I.L.). In the early 1930s Ontarian John T. Smith bought the property after one of his annual hunting trips up Mill Hill. He brought his wife and daughters to live here in 1936, and bought another 25 acres on Mill Hill almost at once.

A daughter, Jimmy Mabb, and her husband live in the house built with bricks from the old powder magazine, well screened by trees from neighbouring commercial enterprises. Her father once owned land up Colwood

hill as far as the Pollock farm, some bought from Baron Strellendorf. "The baron was well-to-do but an unsuccessful gambler. He needed money so he sold his house and his architect-designed chicken house to my father. The baron heard, soon after the sale, that he had inherited a considerable sum of money that would have paid his gambling debts."

The palatial chicken house gained notoriety later when it became known as the 'chicken house motel.' Most people who saw the squalid eyesore towards the end of its life believed it was full of fleas, filth and petrified chicken droppings. Never, says Jimmy Mabb, was it ever inhabited by a single chicken.

"It was designed by an architect for an owner with more money than sense. There was everything a chicken could need, including automatic irrigation, with living quarters for a hired hand between two long wings for the hens. But it was never used. When the owner got the architect's bill he nearly had a heart attack and couldn't afford to pay for it. It was built with lumber better than any used for houses for people, re-

The Hamilton Powder Company wagon in front of the brick powder magazine which stood next to the blacksmith shop at Parson's Bridge. The photo probably dates from the early 1900s. (BCARS 56830)

The Mabbs' house, built partly with bricks from the old magazine. It backs onto the upper reaches of Esquimalt Harbour. (Robert Duffus photo)

ally solid. There was even a huge cast-iron shell grinder, like a heavy meat grinder with a huge wheel.

"But best of all there was enough room under one end of the chicken house to tape lines for a tennis court. My honorary uncle Mr. Brulotte, who rented from fa-

ther, and I used to play there all year round, it was so dry and warm. It might have been Victoria's first indoor tennis court." The Smiths lived in the centre part of the chicken house until their house down the hill was completed. The building was turned into a motel shortly after Mr. Smith sold it.

Jimmy and her older sister came out before their parents moved here permanently. They lived in Effie Atkins' old cottage on Hart Road. There was no indoor plumbing or electricity, and they learned to cook on an old wood stove. They got to know Effie well and found her a remarkable character.

Jimmy Mabb remembers the friendliness of the people in the neighbourhood from the time she was a schoolgirl taking the bus to Craigflower School, and the seven-passenger jitney into town. "This was before there were any real buses, and they would stop and wait if they saw regular passengers coming. Everybody talked all the way into town, and there was a constant babble of conversation amongst people from Metchosin or Happy Valley."

Effie Atkins — Horse Trainer and Milliner

Jimmy Mabb remembers: "Mrs. Atkins kept cows on the Hart Road property, which went back to the present defence department fence and down to the waterfront.

"Effie kept her harness-racing horses on pasture above the old quarry. She and Owen, whom she married late in life, really knew how to manage horses, and their thoroughbreds were some of the best in town.

"They had an old plough horse called Jerry. Effie told me the story of Jerry's service for the Department of National Defence. When DND bought the property at the end of Hart Road and Wilfert Road for a magazine before World War II they had trouble getting a fence over the rocks because they couldn't get a truck up. So Effie and her brother Ed said they could do it. They hitched up Jerry, loaded the heavy roles of chain link fence onto an old stone boat that happened to be around, and hauled them up. Effie maintained she had to do it herself, 'or it wouldn't be done properly.'

To many older Victorians, Effie was better known as a milliner. "She and Minnie Beveridge were the only milliners in town, you had to get hats from one or the other," Jimmy recalled. "She first worked as a milliner at the David Spencer department store, but set out on her own when Eaton's bought out the Spencers. Her first shop was opposite the Bay, then she moved to Fisgard, west of Douglas. She had real flair. Tall, slender and independent, with a wonderful carriage. When she dressed up she looked as if she'd stepped straight out of Vogue.

"My husband and I used to play cards with Effie and Owen, and he used to recite the Bible in Welsh. I helped feed and look after the horses if Effie was sick, but she and Owen knew more about horses than most of the experts."

Effie Atkins, later Mrs. Owen Lloyd, was the daughter of Mr. and Mrs. Tommy Atkins. She and her brothers lived on Hart Road behind one of the limestone quarries worked by their father and uncle who founded the business in the 1880s. (Dolly McInnes photo)

Effie Atkins Lloyd's house high on the rocks above her father's old lime quarry, beside the pasture for her horses. (Gladys Durrant drawing)

The Sausage Factory

Across the Inlet, between the Six Mile House and the Galloping Goose trail, Jimmy remembered a sausage factory but couldn't remember who owned it. Mrs. Marion Pitt, who still lives on the property, knows all about the sausages and pork pies produced in the little plant by the water's edge:

"After my husband and I came to live here in the late 20s my father, Ernest Goucher, set up the business. His family used to own a large butcher shop in Manchester. An old photograph shows the large staff, about 20 people, in front of a sign saying 'By Appointment' to some royalty. The firm was famous for its pork pies, called Melton Mowbray. When we came to Canada in 1908 Dad bought land in Langford and built greenhouses to start a nursery business. But the great snow of 1916 knocked them flat, so he went into various other businesses, including showing movies in a hall on the property which also served for church services.

"In the late 20s Dad still knew how to make excellent pies and sausages in a building down by the water. He was very ingenious and made a sort of water wheel on the stream that ran through our property from Thetis Lake, under the old CN tracks. This gave enough power to run the compressor for his refrigeration plant. He made some sort of pulley and rope arrangement for lifting the cases up the steep bank from the cold storage house to his delivery car. I know he supplied some of the best hotels, including the Empress, with large pies, as big as a dinner plate. I used to help stuff the sausages into their casings, so I'm still not much of a sausage lover."

Mrs. Pitt and her husband owned 12 acres of land between the Six Mile House and the CN tracks but sold the lots along Chilco before he died in 1960. Mr. Pitt was a well-known pianist who played at the Empress Hotel and the Crystal Garden, and in the orchestra at Chez Marcel.

An old Atkins lime kiln on Hart Road, now almost hidden by a tangle of blackberry bushes with a tree growing up through it. (Robert Duffus photo, 1977)

She remembers the kindness of Mrs. Newham, whose husband was caretaker at the old powder plant before Jimmy's family bought the property. "Mrs. Newham was the belle of Parson's Bridge. She lived where the antique place is. She cheated at gin rummy, but I didn't mind because she was the only one who would play cards with me when I was a child. She adored men, didn't like women, but had a heart as big as the world. She never locked her doors, and anyone could walk in and use the telephone and leave money in a tin on the wall. My parents thought so much of her. When they came on their first hunting trip they thought they could stay at the Six Mile Hotel, not realizing it was just a beer parlour then. They were sent across to Mrs. Newham who gave up a bed for them, and they didn't know until later that she had just come out of hospital."

Other characters on Hart Road were Emil Theriault, known as Frenchy, who used to take off in an old touring car with 'Pa' Newham, who drove at a top speed of 20 miles an hour; Ed Atkins, who worked at the quarry at the corner of Hart Road and the highway; Fred Atkins, the second son, and his wife Emily, who lived next to the Newhams.

"Then there was Mr. Salmond, the original owner of the oyster bed near Parson's Bridge. He was a well-educated Englishman who dressed meticulously in well-tailored suits and drove a Rover with leather interior, all very posh - but his house, right beside Mellor Road, was a pig sty. He used newspapers for table cloths but didn't bother to remove the old ones, so when someone went in to clean after he left they found the 'tablecloths' went back quite a way."

The highway, a cement road with seams every few yards as far as Parson's bridge, was a gravel road to Colwood Corners as late as the 1940s.

Farther up the road were the Fishers. I. J. J. Fisher had an orchard where his grandson, Bob, built the little roadside stand in the early 1950s that became the popular Bob's Burgers. There is a Chinese restaurant there now.

The highway scene changed abruptly at the beginning of World War II when the acute housing shortage for military families led to construction of five or six motels, home to servicemen and their families, and later catering to tourists. The story goes that one of the motels was hastily built of lumber from the stands of the old Colwood race track.

Across the highway from Bob's Burgers were the Pollock greenhouses and beyond that a piggery. The late Roger Couche bought the pig farm and built his restaurant, Chez Marcel, in the early 1950s. People came from all over Victoria to his popular dinner dance evenings. The car dealership now on the site marks the end of the View Royal part of Highway 1A.

Jimmy Mabb also remembers the sailing ship master, Captain Lund, who owned land at the north end of Chilco Road, and the Chinese market garden on the

Swans at the edge of former asparagus field, below the Harle house, where lumber was loaded onto scows from the H.B.C. mill in the 1850s. (Duffus Collection)

old Thetis Lake Road where her family bought fresh vegetables.

On Atkins Road west of Chilco, Oswald Harle had an all-purpose farm, bought from the Hudson's Bay Company in the 1920s. He grew asparagus on the flats at the head of Esquimalt Harbour and had his mink sheds in the upper field. A later owner, Jack Aylwin, turned it into a profitable mink ranch. It still supports a small flock of sheep and one or two horses. Dick Rant remembers the swimming hole below the Harle's house, and recognizes the tree hanging out over the water. Boys in the 1930s used to swing out on a rope and drop into the water at high tide. A younger generation used the same tree in the 1970s.

Skating with the Patricks

Across the road from the Pollock fields is the cottage that belonged to Matt Fagan, and some of his 80-year-old apple trees still produce old-fashioned 'organic' apples.[31] He is best known in Victoria as the 'honorary grandfather' of dozens of young skaters he instructed after he retired and had time to switch from hockey to figure skating.

He was born in Ireland and came to North America as a child. His father homesteaded first in South Dakota and came to Victoria as section foreman with the E.&N. when Matt was 13. He and his brother went to Craigflower School where Matt won the roll of honour (for high marks in 1894) which hangs in the restored schoolhouse. He started work on the railway in 1895 as a wiper and is listed as an engineer sometime around 1899. He took some of the first trains to Courtney and Port Alberni.

In the early days Mr. Fagan skated with the Patrick brothers, Lester and Frank, at the old Patrick Arena. He took up figure skating after he retired in 1941 and was a regular member of the Victoria Figure Skating Club. He was made an honorary member of the Canadian Figure Skating Association in recognition of his work with young skaters. To keep in shape for skating he swam a circle around Thetis Lake daily until he was 80, and at different times saved two people from drowning. He died in 1973 at the age of 94.

Next to the Fagan orchard was a tannery owned by an Italian called Mr. Esposito. Bob Granderson had the farm next to the tannery, and the late Bill Donelly kept sheep there until he sold it for the development of Myra Place. Across the road was another piggery. View Royal ends at the top of the hill where the old CN tracks used to cross on the way to Sooke. The land behind, up the slopes of Mill Hill, is designated land reserve for future residential needs.

Engineer Matt Fagan in an undated photograph by George Crocker. (Don MacLachlan collection)

Matt Fagan lived in his Atkins Road house, surrounded by 100 apple trees, for 54 years. (Gladys Durrant drawing)

---

31   There is a story that the many old apple trees along Atkins Road and the Galloping Goose trail grew from seeds scattered by Tommy Atkins, the Johnny Appleseed of View Royal, as he walked along the trails to his lime quarries.

Farm Under Glass

The Pollock Brothers' 'farm under glass' was featured in a front page story in the March 17, 1927, edition of *Farm and Home*, "The Great Farm Journal of British Columbia."

"Specialists in Hothouse Crops Have Placed Historic Ground Adjacent to Victoria Under Glass - Was Site of Ancient Grist Mill" is the long subhead over writer John MacMurchy's byline. The writer describes the farm as he saw it then:

"About six years ago the Pollock brothers purchased a few acres of land at Parson's Bridge from the Hudson's Bay Company. It was heavily wooded and dotted with stumps that required a great deal of powder and horsepower to remove, but they cleared it and put it in condition to produce crops that return a steady income, summer and winter."

When they bought the land in 1922 "it was overgrown with underbrush and infested with stumps as broad as King Arthur's table." Even after it was cleared and put under crop "the soil was soggy and sometimes flooded, but ... they have laid more than one mile of tile drains under four and one-half acres, and they are now installing additional drains under their glasshouses.

"The energy and powder that it cost to clear the place was enormous but the outcome has justified the expenditure. Beds of flowers, houses full of plants, rows of garden truck, and a steady succession of something to sell are repaying these men for what they have done ... They market their own produce and find a good demand for good products.

"Every month in the year there is a gorgeous array of color around this place. Just now the daffodils, tulips, lily of the valley and sweet-scented white stevia are brightest in the houses. The Spanish and Dutch iris are coming along and it is only a few weeks since the full

Summer flowers, nearly as high as the verandah rail, were cut for sale in the shop run by Malcolm's wife Agnes. (Pollock collection)

Produce from the Pollock farm was first sold at their stall in the old Victoria Market behind City Hall. They opened their own store, Pollock's Florists at 1315 Douglas Street in 1934. H. U. Knight photo, ca. 1929-30. (City of Victoria Archives)

houses of chrysanthemums finished blooming. Thousands of dozens of daffodils are forced here every winter and a succession of blooms maintained over a period of many weeks by a systematic manipulation of the bulbs ... Within and without the little farm is bright with blossoms ..."

Malcolm Pollock "was one of the first to mush over the passes and enter the gold fields of the Klondike in 1897," MacMurchy wrote. "He was in that country before the trail of '98 was worn bare by the thousands of searchers that followed." But he had always loved growing things and soon left the gold fields. His brother Neil came to B. C. a few years later and learned the wholesale fruit and produce business during seven years with F. R. Stewart and Company. He was a member of various agricultural organizations,

and "a keen business man [who] puts as much system in his selling as he does in his producing."

The houses had an advanced heating system consisting of "two Robin Hood boilers, made in England, and installed in such a way that each boiler heats two houses." The cooling system and ventilation were also state of the art "... as Neil Pollock claims that the flavor of tomatoes is influenced by the amount of good clean oxygen that gets to them during their period of growth." The writer notes that Neil Pollock was "right on so many things he's probably right on this too."

Generations of Victorians remember Pollock tomatoes, bought at the farm or at Pollock's Florists on Douglas Street as the gourmet tomato of all time. Regular customers could also buy fresh milk and eggs at the florists.

Agnes Pollock. (Pollock collection)

Neil and Malcolm Pollock at an agricultural conference, ca. 1940. (Pollock collection)

"They have four glass-houses covering an area of over 15,500 square feet." Third generation Pollock, David, whose parents Earl and Phyllis Pollock took over the business after the brothers retired, in one of the large greenhouses, early 1950s. (David Pollock collection)

Notes For Garden Clubs

A list of some of the old varieties of tomatoes and flowers, and some horticultural advice, might be useful for gardeners interested in heritage plants and seeds.

Stable manure was used in large quantities and some blood, bone and superphosphate were added, especially for the tomato crop. "The phosphatic manures seem to have an important role in the production of firm bright, early fruits and heavy yields," the brothers claimed. Some of the varieties grown in the 1920s

were Sutton's Best of All, Balsh's Gem and the non-acid French Marvel. "We still grow French Marvel," David Pollock says, "even though it doesn't give the heavy yield of newer hybrids."

Between the Canadian Tire store and a car dealership on Colwood hill is a field which used to be part of the Pollock farm where a few daffodils still bloom each spring, the descendants of rejected bulbs dumped in the fields when the greenhouses were cleaned out. Daffodil varieties included Princeps, Golden Spur, King Alfred, Emperor, Victoria, Poeticus Ornat and Laurens Koster. Tulips included Clara Butt, Princess

Elizabeth, Madam Krelag and Professor Rauenhauf. Every year the succession of blooms was kept up until after Mother's Day.

Sixty-six years ago, according to *Farm and Home*, there were also "two vast beds of Mastodon pansies" which "occupy a spot so historic that it might be considered hallowed ground. They bloom at the top of the ravine in which, immediately below, the first oatmeal on the Pacific coast was made."

Although part of the property was sold when the Colwood strip was zoned for commercial use, the family still farms the land across Millstream, continuing to keep cattle for a good supply of manure for the tomatoes, corn and other vegetables grown by Malcolm Pollock's son Earl.

Grandson David Pollock and his wife Ingelese planted a 300-tree apple orchard in 1990, nearly 70 years after the Pollock Brothers first began to clear the land. David writes:

The Pollock brothers are gone. Neil died in 1949 and Malcolm in 1959. Regrettably the greenhouses, after standing for 50 years, are gone too. But the waters still flow through 'Kelvin Grove' over a waterfall which changes daily yet remains the same as it was centuries ago. Douglas firs which were saplings when Champlain sailed for New France preside over the humble activities of those who live and work on the land below.

Our property is home to eagles, Canada geese, deer who would eat our orchard trees, and even the occasional cougar who might eat the deer if left alone. We have also kept cattle for more than 60 years. It is an enclave reminiscent of a simpler time and that is how we would like it to stay.

Top, Haying behind the greenhouses, 1948. Middle, hay stacks on site of the Canadian Tire parking lot, Old Island Highway at Wilfert Road. Bottom, the dairy house, still standing on the bank above Millstream Falls. (Pollock collection)

The Wilfert Mill

Peter Cox

In 1926-27 Frank Wilfert dismantled a Campbell River sawmill and had it transported to Esquimalt Harbour where he had it re-erected on the west side of the harbour near the present naval fuelling jetty. Mr. Piercy had charge of erecting the mill on the harbour site and remained head millwright during the life of the mill.

It was steam-powered and used headrig sawdust for fuel. It was referred to as a double head rig mill, with the circular main saws mounted vertically, one above the other. Mill capacity averaged 60,000 to 70,000 board feet daily, the majority for export. The average work force was around 25. Some wood waste was sold to firewood dealers, the rest was burned.

The Rout Of The Pile Drivers

For many years vast log booms filled Esquimalt Harbour as far as Cole Island. Long after the smoke from the Wilfert mill disappeared the log booms remained as visual pollution. The booms grew larger and encroached closer to the residential shore until one day in the 1960s three ladies taking their early morning dip found pile drivers within a few feet of the shore. Courageously, they boarded the 'Comtesse de Barfleur,' rowed straight to the intruding machine, and vowed to stay until the villains moved away. Since then, the log booms have been kept far away across the harbour. The heroines' names? No record has been found, but the historic incident is remembered. The heritage rowboat is preserved on a nearby waterfront property. (Robert Duffus photo)

The Oyster Beds

The earliest record of an oyster lease in Esquimalt Harbour is a handwritten notation on an 1858 map. The undated addition shows Alfred Markham had a lease southwest of Thetis Cove. The first reference to the bed near Parson's Bridge came from Elsie Plowright whose brother, John Donaldson, seeded an oyster bed near there in 1908. The oysters were brought in by railway from the east. According to Jimmy Mabb a Mr. Salmond was the original owner of the present oyster bed started in the early 30s. Dave McMillan took over later, and the oysters were said to be top quality. The old shed has been abandoned and rotting for more than 40 years. (William E. John photo, circa 1968)

Vanished Burger Heavens

Second and third generation View Royalites have their memories, too. Especially of places to eat. Two of the most memorable post-war eateries were Bob's Burgers and Big Ben's. Bob's Burgers started as a roadside stand on what had been Bob Fisher's grandfather's orchard. It was an ideal spot on the Old Island Highway across from the Pollock greenhouses, and the burgers and soft ice cream were superb. The little wooden stand evolved into a drive-in restaurant before it was sold. Bob Fisher built the house high on a hill behind the restaurant and garden ornament shop.

Polar Pete's ice cream bar was near the present Six-Mile Market. David Pollock remembers walking down the hill with his grandfather to buy that greatest of ice cream treats, a Revel.

A gas station and car wash have supplanted a series of restaurants next to the Six Mile House, including the House of Chan, the House of Lee and the Six-Mile Cafe operating since the 40s when cheeseburgers were the greatest. The Red Rooster was a little cafe beside the View Royal garage, and there was a cabaret at the top of the Four Mile hill for a short time. Val's fish and chips shop was nearby.

> **BIG BEN'S BURGERS** – Plain **35c**, Spanish Onion **40c**,
> Cheese **40c**, Tomato **40c**, with everything **45c**,
> Coney **45c**, Turkey **60c**, Deep Sea **40c**, Oyster **55c**,
> Big Ben's Beefy Boy **55c**.

Dropping in for lunch, this helicopter brought a work crew from a far-off logging or highways project to Bob's Burgers ca. 1974. (Robert Duffus photo)

Long distance swimmer Ben Laughren was one of the owners of the drive-in that stood in front of Craigflower Farmhouse in its neglected days. The 35-cent burgers and 10-cent root beer at Big Ben's Burger Boulevard were famous throughout the district. Ben sold the drive-in to the Dog and Suds in 1964. It was eventually demolished along with the nearby service station and Discovery Motel when the heritage value of the old farmhouse was recognized. (William E. John photos, ca. 1962)

View Royal Churches

The 82-year-old St. Columba Church, first heated with wood and coal stove stoked by sidesmen, was lit by coal oil lamps. The stained glass window showing St. Columba leaving Ireland for the Isle of Iona was presented in 1986 by parish treasurer Dr. Bill English and his sister in memory of their parents. (Robert Duffus Photo)

The earliest church services were conducted in Craigflower Schoolhouse by Hudson's Bay Company or Royal Navy chaplains. Later, the Four Mile House served as a meeting place, as did community halls.

St. Columba Church

(Excerpts from a history of St. Columba Church compiled by Mrs. H. J. Newnham and Miss L. Feesey)

Until St. Columba Church was built in 1912 Anglicans of the Strawberry Vale area had to walk two miles along a cow trail to an old hall at Colquitz, according to notes on the history of the church compiled by Mrs. H. J. Newnham.

She mentions C. B. Jones, P. James and John Clapperton as some of the first fundraisers for a local church, and notes that Miss Elliot donated the property at the corner of High Street and Burnside. A. Gaunt, an architect and member of the congregation, drew up the plans. Building contractors Burnham and Holmes had the church ready for its first service on October 8, 1912, when 116 people attended. Those who arrived by horse and buggy stabled their horses in the shed at the community hall. Miss Mable Gaunt was at the organ, Miss Kitty Walker was violinist, and a full choir was led by Mrs. Hilda Dawson. There was Sunday school for the young people, and many Christmas parties and summer picnics by hay wagon.

The font for the first infant baptism was a tree stump brought in for use as a stand for Mrs. Gaunt's cut glass bowl, which she loaned to the church for Lawrence

Ball's christening. Mr. Gaunt and Mr. Foster made the first pews and the pulpit; Mr. H. James donated the lectern, Mr. Garford-Beaumont made the first hymn boards and a patient from the mental home made the notice board. The church bell, an old train bell, was added several years later.

Bishop Scriven dedicated the church a year later. St. Columba and St. Michael and All Angels, Royal Oak, two formed a parish separate from St. Luke's. Rev. H. B. Hadlow was first incumbent of the new parish.

The Women's Auxiliary dated back to 1907 with meetings held in members' homes or at the Colquitz Hall. The Women's Guild worked tirelessly to raise money "to free the church from debt ... organizing suppers, socials and concerts ... all of which contributed much to the social life of the Burnside residents."

In 1926 Mrs. A. Gaunt donated the piece of land adjoining the church property for the parish hall.

The 25th anniversary of St. Columba Church was celebrated October 10, 1937, with Rev. Robert Connell preaching at the 11:00 a.m. service and the rector, Canon S. J. Wickens, at the evening service.

The original foundations were found to be subsiding unevenly during a 1961 check, so a new basement was built and an automatic oil furnace installed. The new basement provided room for a Sunday school, and a robing room for the choir for the first time.

The parishes of St. Columba and All Saints, View Royal, were joined in 1963 with Rev. John Vickers as rector. The combined choirs of the two churches sang at the impressive induction service at All Saints on October 30.

All Saints Church

Michael Pope

St. Columba was the only Anglican Church in the district until 1943, when several people in the southern part of View Royal felt there should be another closer to the growing population.

Arrangements were made with the Four Mile House to use an upper room for services for a monthly cost of $5. The first service was held there May 3, 1943, conducted by Rev. K. Sandercock, rector of St. Martin in-

The bell tower of All Saints Church, View Royal. (Michael Pope photo)

the-Field, for a congregation of 22. The View Royal Anglican Church, as it was called then, was officially organized as a congregation on October 3, 1943. The following year the View Royal Welfare Association, which controlled the newly-built Community Hall, allowed use of the hall for church services every Sunday from 10 to 11 a.m. The modest rent was $5 a month.

Canon Greenhalgh took over from Mr. Sandercock in August, 1945, and served until 1948 when he was replaced by Canon S. J. Wickens. Plans for a new church were progressing, and minutes of the 1951 annual vestry meeting list suggested names: St. Augustine, St. James, St. Philip and St. Jude. Apparently none was acceptable. At the next annual meeting the rector mentioned that "this is the first meeting where we are meeting as a congregation with a name." The church was now known as All Saints. That year a lot was purchased on Pallisier Avenue for $1,000. There were grumbles from many who felt that this was a lot of money to spend for a lot of rock.

The Ladies Guild was formed in 1952 with Mrs. Marjorie Reynolds as first president. The guild was active in fundraising projects for the new building. Garden parties, church suppers, teas and other events helped swell the building fund. Mr. Goldring, who lived in the large old Holden house, opened his garden for fundraising activities organized by the guild. In appreciation he was made an official member of the Ladies Guild, much to his delight.

The decision to go ahead with building was made at the 1953 annual meeting. An architect, Mr. J. Wilson, was commissioned to produce plans, which the parish-

ioners approved, and on July 20, 1954, Darcy Construction was awarded the contract to build the church. The last service in the community hall was held February 20, 1955. The first service and dedication were held in the new church the following Sunday, February 27. Fundraising was so successful that the church was paid for in three years. The parish hall was completed by 1963.

Fundraising continues. The Ladies Guild, the Sunday school, the Anglican Church Women and other organizations are active, and the Bargain Centre, open every Saturday morning in the parish hall basement, raises money for general funds.

Old Ship's Bell Calls Congregation

Phyllis McAdams and Michael Pope

Each Sunday the bell of the beautiful little Church of All Saints, cradled on a rocky knoll not far from the sea, calls forth the View Royal congregation. Its plain ding-dong cannot be expected to sound like melodious music, for it was created to clang out the hours of the watch on a sailing vessel built in Dumbarton, Scotland, in 1893.

The *Blairmore*, a steel barque 294 feet fore and aft with a 40-foot beam, was used in the charter market. In February, 1896, she arrived in San Francisco with a cargo of coal. After unloading she remained at anchor in Mission Bay until April 9 when a squall struck the big square-rigger. The southwest wind caught her broadside and she heeled over. Her master, Captain John Caw, refused assistance but the ship, empty ex-

The old ship's bell still rings clear from the bell tower of the church, out to sea as it did when it was new and polished on its voyage from England 100 years ago. (Michael Pope collection)

cept for 260 tons of ballast, took on water through her hatches and sank with the loss of several lives.

She was raised eventually as she was a danger to navigation, and towed by a nearby dock where she remained for several months. She was renamed the *Abby Palmer* after she was repaired and put back in service. She underwent another name change when she was sold to Alaska Packers and became the *Star of England*. Then for a while the bell was silent. The ship had been sold to a group of monied people who fitted her out richly for a treasure hunt. But this turned out to be only a dream. She never set sail for any treasure isles.

In 1935 the Island Tug and Barge Company of Victoria bought the vessel in San Francisco and brought her to Victoria. Reluctantly they stripped her of her rich trappings and dismantled her masts, rigging and decks. The once proud ship became a chip barge renamed the *Island Star*, running out of Port Alberni. The barge was later sold to Crown Zellerbach and worked out of Ocean falls and New Westminster before coming to an ignoble end. She was scrapped sometime around 1960.

The bell, deprived of ship, became the prized possession of Harold Elworthy of Island Tug and Barge. When Duncan McTavish told his old friend that the View Royal church was in need of a bell Mr. Elworthy fitted it out with a ringing device and presented it to the church in 1955, along with a picture of the ship best known as the *Abby Palmer*.

Shakers as Healers

(Excerpts from an article by T. W. Paterson in The Daily Colonist, August 8, 1971)

The little wood frame Shaker church, a curious landmark beside Craigflower Road for nearly half a century, combined a mixture of Christianity and Indian beliefs in its healing rituals. The ceremonies were brought from Washington State Indian practices to the Songhees reserve that was once part of View Royal. Founder of the sect was a member of the Puget Sound Squaxin Tribe, John Slocum.

The late Wilson Duff, a B.C. anthropologist, described its beginnings in his Indian History of British Columbia, Vol. 1. In the early 1880s Slocum recovered from a near-fatal illness, convinced that he had been chosen by God to save his fellow tribesmen. He had been assigned the earthly task of "preaching to the Indian people so that they might get to heaven."

The unusual form of worship took its name from the shaking attributed to Slocum's wife's violent trembling after she had nursed him through another serious illness. This miraculous healing was considered a sign of divine intervention, so the Shaker Church was formed. Converts throughout the northwest were noted for their ritual of trembling from head to heel to cure sick people.

The Craigflower church is believed to have been built about the turn of the century. Another was built at West Saanich. Times reporter Humphry Davy described a healing service:

" ... the electric lights are put out and the candles lit. Then the congregation joins in prayers and hymns in their native tongue. This is followed by chanting and the ringing of bells to a beat. The brass hand bells are rung vigorously while the congregation stamp their feet and dance.

"Those endeavouring to help the ailing person may suddenly develop the shakes - that is, involuntary trembling from head to foot. They dance and brush against the patient to draw the illness out. To members of the congregation, the shakes emanate from God ... "

The Craigflower church had been abandoned for many years when it was bulldozed to make more room in the reserve's mobile home park. Before its final demise it was used by local youngsters as a leaky-roofed floor hockey arena. Attempts to move the old ruins and restore them as a community recreation hall were abandoned when it was found to be too far gone. The steeple, for many years minus the cross-arm of its cross, resisted to the last.

Meeting Places

The 100-year-old Strawberry Vale Hall. (Robert Duffus photo)

Strawberry Vale Community Hall

(From notes provided by Richard Moyer, historian of the
Strawberry Vale and District Community Club)

Land for a meeting place for the residents of Strawberry Vale was donated by the late Percival Ridout Brown in 1890. The hall was built by volunteers, of materials freely donated, between 1890 and 1893. Some who helped with building were James Barker and his son James Henry, and Samuel Huston. Material and other help was donated by T. R. Porter,

James Daley and John McNeill, who became the first trustees of the property.

Crowds from as far away as Metchosin arrived in buggies for the first dances in the hall. Sam Scafe's orchestra played, and Mrs. A. E. Longland remembered the opening dance when her mother, Mrs. Miller, led the grand march and T. R. Porter danced a highland schottishe.

The original hall served the community well for more than 50 years. But by 1947 it was in sad condition and there were substantial rumours threatening closure and dismantling. There was no proper foundation. The building rested on old posts and stone slabs. Plumbing consisted of one cold water tap outside, and the building leaned badly. The old horse stables at the north end were a dangerous shambles.

The first meeting toward formation of a community club was held in December, 1947, at the instigation of Mrs. Doreen Jones, chairman of the playground group then using the premises for the younger children of the district. The Strawberry Vale and District Community Club was incorporated in 1948 and title was transferred to the club that year.

After nearly half a century of hard work and countless hours of voluntary labour providing professional workmanship, the club has one of the finest community halls in Victoria. All directors work on a voluntary basis and the historic hall is used and enjoyed by hundreds of people who live far beyond the community boundaries.

There are many tales of well-known characters of Strawberry Vale, which includes land in Saanich as well as View Royal. Mr. Moyer has collected many of

At a pioneer dinner at Strawberry Vale Community Hall in 1964, 17-year-old Juanita Warren wore a dress that had been worn by her grandmother, Mrs. Margaret Miller, to the first dance at the hall in 1895. The dress was brown taffeta trimmed with gold embroidery. (Strawberry Vale Community Club collection)

these in a history based on interviews with old-timers over the years since 1961. The club has collected records and photographs from early days, and owns some paintings by the late Captain Alcock, a well-known resident.

The Alcock house on Eaton Avenue. (Gladys Durrant drawing)

The View Royal Community Hall

(From notes from Al Beasley, Shirley Wade and others)

The little hall at 279 Old Island Highway was built as an A.R.P. centre to provide fire protection during World War II. It was completed in 1943 with some financial help from the provincial government and a lot of volunteer labour. Equipment for the

Jim Pilgrim and Alec McKay with two representatives of the provincial government in front of the nearly-completed A.R.P. centre, 1943. (Pilgrim collection)

volunteer firemen consisted of steel helmets and coveralls, and a hose and hose-reel.

This was the only fire protection until 1948 when the View Royal Volunteer fire department was formed. A. E. (Al) Beasley was appointed fire chief and served for 21 years until 1969. The first volunteers were recruited from a local softball team known as "The District Merchants." The first fire truck consisted of a 300-gallon water tank mounted on a truck bought from local resident George Wilmshurst. It was housed at Cyril Parson's garage, then at the home of deputy fire chief Alwyn Trace.

On March 4, 1950, sod was turned for an addition at the back of the community hall to house the fire truck. The hall was fire department headquarters until a new fire hall was built across the highway on property bought from Bill Duval.

The A.R.P. hall became the community hall at the end of the war, and still serves as a centre for many community activities, including the View Royal library, meetings of the ratepayers' association which now owns the building, and the Craigflower Women's Institute.

The All-Volunteer Library

Phyllis McAdams

More than 10,000 books fill the shelves in the lower rooms of the community hall. The View Royal Library Association is independent of the Greater Victoria Public Library and the Vancouver Island Regional Library, and has always been operated entirely by volunteers.

The first library service in View Royal was organized by Mr. and Mrs. C. A. Pope who arranged to have the provincial government travelling library bring books to the community. These and some donated volumes

were the beginnings of the library in one small room at the community hall.

The collection has been built up since 1971 when money was raised by the projects committee of the View Royal Community Centre in one of the lower rooms provided by the View Royal Ratepayers Association. Renovation of the room was made possible by a provincial government Centennial 71 grant.

At first the library was open two days a week, and library membership was $1 a year for each family.

Money was scarce and the shelves filled slowly. As public interest grew opening hours were extended. There was never a lack of volunteer workers. Raffles, arts and crafts sales, plant sales and sales of duplicate and discarded books - and fines - brought in extra money for buying books. Bargain books at Goodwill sales were much sought after.

The View Royal Parks and Recreation Commission provided funds in 1977, and the membership fee was raised to $2. Since View Royal became a town in 1988 a yearly municipal grant provides funds and the room which once housed the volunteer fire department equipment has been taken over for the growing collection.

There are now more than 30 volunteers, some of whom have been donating time since 1971. The friendly atmosphere of the library welcomes the ever-growing number of readers, including children who browse happily in the well-stocked children's corner. The service is free to all View Royal residents.

Charles Arthur Pope arranged the first library service in View Royal in 1943. (Michael Pope collection)

The Craigflower Women's Institute

(Notes from Shirley Wade, daughter of founding member Myrtle Pilgrim)

As more families with young children moved to View Royal in the 1930s, the mothers felt isolated in the rural community. Houses were far apart, telephones were scarce and the need for company great. Though they met informally for coffee and sharing child-minding, picnics and swimming parties, they began to think about a more formal association. It was chance that led them to the Women's Institute movement.

Someone suggested they should get in touch with a WI organizer to find out more about the organization. Myrtle Pilgrim and Mary Fieldhouse knocked on doors from central View Royal to the Indian Reserve, scooping up as many women as they could for a tea and meeting in the old Craigflower Schoolhouse. To

"I'm having a tea" was the signal for young wives and mothers of the isolated community of south View Royal to get dressed up for a party. This 1930 photo shows a party for Mrs. Diment, who was moving away. Guests included Doris Hawthorne, Stevie Stevenson (a niece of Amy Stewart), Amy Stewart, Mrs. Dan Stewart, Mrs. Jean McTavish, Mrs. Sheard, Myrtle Pilgrim, Virginia Goodman, Isabel Goodman and Mrs. Willy Hall, surrounding Mrs. Diment, centre. (Pilgrim collection)

A 1937 photo shows the original members of the Craigflower Women's Institute. Back row, left to right, are Myrtle Pilgrim, Jean ('Granny') MacLeod, Lil Burnett, unknown, Vi Bligh, Bubbsy Phillips with a child, Joyce Albany, Ethel Rankin and Ivy Waring with baby Ann. Seated at the table are Claire Allen, Millie Gouge, unknown, and Inez Pearson with Velva. Left, front, is Mary Warren, Joyce Albany's mother, and Ethel Hudson, centre. (Pilgrim collection)

their suprise, 34 prospective members turned up, and the Craigflower Women's Institute was formed. The WI motto, For Home and Country, suited them well.

By 1939 the members found their talents were needed for the war effort. They organized First Aid classes, manned a civil defence post, gave out ration books, and began sewing and knitting for 'Bundles for Britain.' They also created recipes to stretch rations, and produced a stage show for the entertainment of troops stationed at Esquimalt.

They continued to meet at the old school but planned to build their own hall eventually, hoping to buy prop-erty near Pallisier Avenue. Instead, as the war continued, they bought war bonds with money they raised, then helped with fundraising for the new A.R.P. hall. They have been meeting there ever since.

For 55 years the group, still called the Craigflower Women's Institute, has continued community work, participating in local, provincial and Country Women of the World projects. Meetings are held twice a month and the sewing, knitting and crafts still draw crowds to the popular annual bazaars.

Thetis Lake Park

Lloyd Brooks

One of the most beautiful natural parks in Greater Victoria is within the boundaries of View Royal. Like Thetis Cove in Esquimalt Harbour, it was apparently named for HMS Thetis, a Royal Navy frigate stationed at Esquimalt in 1852.

Thetis Lake Municipal Park, with its 1,533 acres of lakes, streams and timbered hills, forms a major part of the land and water area of the Town of View Royal. In reality it is a park reserve, owned and maintained by the city of Victoria. Like many such large parks it is an accident of geography and jurisdiction, preserved

from developers through the dedicated and persistent efforts of a few visionary individuals.

Most of the area was originally set aside, along with the Elk-Beaver lakes area, as a source of domestic water for the city of Victoria. A private company, the Esquimalt Waterworks, took over the Thetis Lake area in 1885, developing its water storage potential by building an earthen dam in 1887. This, along with other sources, provided water for a growing urban area from 1892 to 1915. The dam raised water levels joining the two major lakes which form the continu-

A trail to the right of the parking lot leads to the remains of the surge reservoir built on the south slope of Seymour Hill, ca. 1885. It is now known as Bladderwort Pond. (Robert Duffus photo)

ous water body that exists today as an attractive recreational feature.

In 1925 the city of Victoria expropriated the undertakings of the Esquimalt Waterworks. This included the 1,100 acres of the Thetis Lake watershed, acquired at a price of $35 per acre or a total of $38,500. It is no longer a part of the Victoria water system, which now relies on the far greater potential of the Sooke Lake/Goldstream watershed.

Thetis Lake was opened to the public in 1932. It was another 43 years before the area received official status of park reserve in 1975, to protect the area from threats of subdivision or resources development. This protection came about mainly through the persistence of a small group registered as the Thetis Lake Nature Sanctuary Association in 1959. Dr. E. H. Lohbrunner was first president. The city of Victoria showed confidence in the association's work by designating 400 acres as a nature sanctuary. The association is responsible for improving trails and studying, protecting and interpreting this key area.

The park reserve came under a number of serious threats over the years, including subdivision expansion, powerline right of ways, logging and highways. The association has been successful in bringing these to the attention of the public and warding of most of these threats. It was also instrumental in persuading the provincial government to buy 424 acres in the northern drainage area which were slated for subdivision in 1980. Highway expansion is probably the current most serious threat.

In colonial days land near the lake was bought by a few settlers, including some of the Hudson's Bay employees when their five year contracts were up. John Greeg or Grieg had a lime-burning operation, of which traces remain, and his cattle grazed nearby. Later members of his family planted some of the old pear trees still growing along the 'blue' trail. Victoria's first mayor Thomas Harris also had grazing land on the western side Thetis Park. In the 1890s water for the Atkins Road brickworks was brought from the lake through a wooden flume.

Swimming at Thetis

One of the many young people who swam at Thetis before it was officially opened to the public was George MacFarlane:

As boys we used to swim in the summer at Thetis Lake because the water was quite warm up there. Thetis Lake in those days was still kept in reserve as part of the Victoria water system, and as such was posted No Trespassing. There was a house there where a caretaker lived and the trick was to sneak in through the woods, round past the caretaker's house so we weren't seen. Once we got to the lake we were probably all right swimming for three or four hours before the caretaker would make his rounds, at which point we would flee out through the woods, get back on the road further up and then make our way home. All the boys in View Royal swam there as far as I can remember every summer. We swam from a high bluff in the early spring on the right hand side of the lake from the dam. We always had a bonfire, the idea being to warm you up after swimming in the cold lake. Summer time when we didn't need a fire we moved down to the opposite side of the lake. We had no fire then because of the danger of starting a forest fire. One summer there was a bad fire on the island on the lake and it was pretty well burned off.

Trees have grown on the little island in Thetis Lake since the unexplained fire in the early 1930s. (Robert Duffus photo)

Craigflower Survives

Maureen Duffus

On Vancouver Island a 140-year-old farm is OLD. Fort Victoria was only 10 years old when Craigflower Farm was begun in 1853. The big white farmhouse was completed in 1855, a remarkable edifice in the little settlement on the edge of the forest.

Craigflower had many tenants after the Puget's Sound Agricultural Company gave it up as a bad investment. Several times it was near death by neglect but survived more by good luck than heritage pride. Its last brush with destruction came shortly after the Provincial Government aquired the property. The old house was in such a deplorable, and dangerous state that former View Royal fire chief Al Beasley ordered it fixed up or he would have to burn it down.

"Croquet, Swings and Quoits"

The first recorded tenant after the McKenzie family moved to Lakehill Farm was Mr. E. C. Holden who recognized a good guest house site when he saw it. He ran the following advertisement in several editions of the Colonist beginning May 12, 1868:

Craigflower House,
Head of Victoria Arm

Mr. E. C. Holden, *late of the St. George Hotel, Victoria City, respectfully informs his friends and the public generally, that he has leased the above property and is prepared to receive a few*

Boarders and Summer Visitors

The House is situated in one of the most beautiful and picturesque spots in the Colony. Fishing, Hunting, Bathing, Boating and every other rural recreation can be indulged in by visitors patronizing this House, and it will be the constant effort of the Proprietor to make the stay of his guests pleasant and agreeable.

The domestic arrangements being under the immediate supervision of Mrs. Holden, lady visitors will receive every attention. The Garden and Grounds are in course of preparation for Croquet, Swings, Quoits, &c. and a convenient landing for Boating Parties is being made.

Refreshments of all kinds (except Wines, Ales and Spirits) furnished at all hours.

The Proprietor, thankful for past favors, trusts that the citizens of Victoria and vicinity will favor him with their kind patronage.

Next came the Parker family who raised 11 children on the farm and ran a dairy farm and slaughter house. Around 1901 to about 1919 the Picock family lived in the house and ran a dairy farm.

H. E. Newton leased it as a camp for young ladies sometime in the late 20s and early 30s. George MacFarlane says it was a nature sanctuary with No Trespassing signs during Newton's tenancy. Then the Hudson's Bay Company used the old house as a men's club, holding card parties and dances for staff of the Douglas Street store.

The house and remaining property passed out of Hudson's Bay Company hands in 1936 when John Christie bought it and Craigflower became a private home again. Christie, for whom Christie Point is named and who built the auto court across Admirals Road, started

It may have been at the time of the HBC staff parties that the original sitting room, office and kitchen were combined to form this dining room with "hunting lodge" decor. The regrettable remodelling was restored to the original configuration by Heritage Properties Branch after careful research. The Moosehead has gone elsewhere. (BCARS 59998)

Craigflower Farmhouse stands at the eastern entrance to View Royal, an impressive heritage building on its original site overlooking the Gorge waterway. (Garry Chater photo)

to restore the building. He recovered some of the original McKenzie furniture including the main dining room pieces, the clothes presses and beds.

After he died the remaining property was transferred to his wife as administrator of the estate. Mrs. Christie sold the present site to William Gordon Mackay in 1956. Other pieces were at one point owned by Shell Oil of Canada who built a service station on the corner. A group of financiers in New York held title to the corner lot for a while. At some point the farmhouse was used as an annex for the overflow of tourists from the motel.

Jean and Gerald Thompson also recognized the heritage value of Craigflower farmhouse. They lived there with their sons, Ian and David, and opened the house to the public for several years.

Phyllis McAdams wrote about the Thompsons soon after they began living with history:

Stepping in past the iron-studded door every visitor felt the lived-in atmosphere of warmth and graciousness of the old home.

"It feels lived in because we really do live in every part of the house," Jean Thompson said. "We sleep in the 1850s high-backed beds, and cook in the fireplace in the big room during the winter months when the house is closed to the public." The big room is the original kitchen-dining room and centre of much social activity. "Chicken roasted on a jackspit, which dates back to 1820, is delicious, and stews cooked in a big iron pot hanging from the crane is stew as it should be. Our sons' friends love to come," she continued. "They much prefer Craigflower to modern rumpus rooms. The Thompsons bought some furniture privately and some was donated, including an 1830s clock with all wooden moving parts, and a child's toy cow made of calf hide, which said 'Moo' at the turn of its head.

One signature in the Thompson's visitors book had more than a passing connection with an earlier Craigflower; Captain L. H. Johnston, then captain of the Empress of Canada, worked for the Picock family some 45 years before his return visit.

Letterhead for John Christie's new 'bungalow court' advertises similar activities to those promoted in Mr. Holden's 1868 advertisement. The auto court stands on land once occupied by McKenzie's bakehouse, smithy and other buildings. (George Fieldhouse collection)

The government bought the house and surrounding fields from Mr. and Mrs. Eric Johnson, and the house was declared a National Historic Site in 1967. It is now restored and furnished as it was in 1860 by B.C. Heritage Properties, working from photographs and records. More McKenzie furniture and belongings have been added to the rooms, and some furniture from the James Stewart family's Craigflower days is in keeping with the period. An almost complete set of china on display testifies to the years of care given by Kenneth and Agnes McKenzie and their chilren.

On special occasions when the house is open to the public actors playing members of the McKenzie family and their servants take visitors back through the years to the days when Craigflower was young.

Craigflower Schoolhouse, across a narrow neck of the Gorge, was also saved from collapse by a few dedicated people. The Native Son's and Daughters, many of whom were former pupils, propped it up in the 1920s when it was sagging badly. They collected memorabilia and kept it going until repair bills escalated beyond their means. Major restoration work has been completed by Heritage Properties and the school is open to the public in summers when volunteers from the Canadiana Costume Museum arrange displays and tours. (Herma Raymond photo)

To See It Now

If you're lucky you might still find a piece of rocky waterfront or a view lot for sale, at about a hundred thousand times the $5 an acre paid by Dr. Helmcken for his rocks and swamps.

Failing that, try to find a public access to one of the beaches. It will probably be partially hidden by blackberry bushes carefully nurtured by neighbouring property owners, but investigate the foot of Beaumont Avenue. Climb down to the rocks where a young Amy Stewart once watched ships sail into the harbour and sailors row over for fresh water. On a clear day you can see past the lighthouse at the harbour entrance, across Juan de Fuca Strait to the magnificent Olympic Mountains.

Or put on your boots and walk down past Peter Calvert's Four Mile House to Portage Park, through the muddy bits to the shore where the Whyomilth and their kin hunted, fished and camped. This is about as close as you can get to the look of the place as young Goodie McKenzie saw it in the 1850s.

If you know a local with a canoe or rowboat ask them to take you to Magazine Island to see what's left of the extraordinary buildings of the 19th century naval ammunition depot.

If you detour off Burnside Road down Quincy Street you can look out over Portage Inlet to 'The Pie' which young Winona Bennett saw when she went to watch the logging trains rumbling by. But here, instead of old oak trees lining the shore you'll see the 'new' highway with, almost any time in the afternoon, Victoria's version of gridlock.

Better still, follow the highway early in the morning to the entrance to Thetis Lake Park and explore the former watershed with its miles of wooded trails along the lakeshore and through the woods.

Most of the farms are gone - there's a large regional hospital on Helmcken where the old dairy farms used to be, and an elementary school on the site of a fox farm. A chain store parking lot covers the fields and greenhouse foundations of the Pollock farm.

Perhaps some day you might take time to leave the highways and see what's left of the woods and streams and country roads that the contributors to this book so fondly remember.

Bibliography

Relevant unpublished manuscripts, memoirs and letters at the B.C. Archives and Record Service (BCARS) include the McKenzie Papers, the Robert Melrose diary, Annie Deans's letters, and papers from an uncatalogued Lands and Works file. A copy of the reminiscences of Dr. John Sebastian Helmcken was lent by a member of the family.

Newspapers:

The Victoria Gazette

The British Colonist (later The Daily Colonist)

The Victoria Times

Hudson's Bay Company and Government Records:

Hudson's Bay Company records

Fort Victoria Post Journal (HBC Archives, U. of Manitoba)

Accounts, correspondence

Fort Victoria Letters

Legislative Council of B.C., Minutes

Vancouver Island House of Assembly, Minutes, 1856-1858

Parks Canada historic photographs section

Land documents, B.C. Surveyor General's office, Victoria

B.C. Heritage Properties library

Capital Regional District manuscripts

Publications

Akrigg, G.P.V & Helen B. Akrigg. *British Columbia Chronicle, 1847-1871*. Vancouver: Discovery Press, 1977

Coyle, Brian C. *The Hudson's Bay Company on Vancouver Island, 1847-1857*. Vancouver: Thesis submitted for MA, Simon Fraser University, 1977.

Cracroft, Sophia. *Lady Franklin Visits the Pacific Northwest,* extracts from letters, ed. by Dorothy Blakey Smith. Provincial Archives of B.C. Memoir, 1974.

Duff, Wilson. *The Fort Victoria Treaties*. B.C. Studies, No. 3, 1969

Duffus, Maureen, ed. *Beyond the Blue Bridge, Stories from Esquimalt.* Victoria: Desktop Publishing,1990.

Fawcett, Edgar. *Some Reminiscences of Old Victoria*. Toronto: William Briggs, 1912

- - - - - *Fort Victoria Letters.* Hudson's Bay Record Society, Vol. XXXII

- - - - - *Guide to the Province of British Columbia.* Victoria: T. N. Hibben & Company, 1877

Harrison, J.F.C. *Early Victorian Britain, 1832-51.* London: Fontana Press, 1989

Helgesen, Marion I. *Footprints, Pioneer Families of the Metchosin District*. Victoria, Metchosin School Museum Society, 1983

Ireland, Willard E. *Title to and Description of the Properties comprising the Esquimalt Naval Base.* BCARS, 1942.

Kluckner, Michael. *Victoria The Way It Was*. North Vancouver: Whitecap Books, 1986

Lamb, W. Kaye. "Early Lumbering in British Columbia." *B.C. Historical Quarterly.* Vol. ii, 1938

- - - - - *Empress to the Orient.* Vancouver Maritime Museum Society, Vancouver. 1991

Longstaff, Major F.V. *Esquimalt Naval Base*. 1942

Lugrin, N. de Bertrand. *The Pioneer Women of Vancouver Island, 1843-1866*. John Hosie, ed. The Women's Canadian Club of Victoria, 1928

McKelvie, B.A. *Pageant of B.C.* Toronto: Thomas Nelson & Sons, Toronto. ND

MacLachlan, Donald F. *The Esquimalt and Nanaimo Railway, the Dunsmuir : The Dunsmuir Years: 1884-1905.* Victoria: B.C. Railway Historical Association, 1986

Mallandaine, Edward. *First Victoria Directory*. Victoria, 1860

- - - - - *Directory for 1863.* Victoria, 1863

Martin, Jed, and Jeffrey Simpson. *Canada's Heritage in Scotland.* Toronto and Oxford: Dundurn Press, 1989

- - - - - *Natural Hitory of Thetis Lake Park.* Thetis Park Nature Sanctuary Association, 1974

Ormsby, Margaret. *British Columbia: A history*. Toronto: Macmillan, 1958

Pethick, Derek. *Victoria: The Fort.* Mitchell Press Limited, Vancouver. 1968

- - - - - *James Douglas: Servant of Two Empires.* Vancouver: Mitchell Press, 1969

Pettit, Sydney. "The Trials and Tribulations of Edward Edwards Langford," *B.C. Historical Quarterly*, Vol. XVII, 1 & 2.

Plasterer, Dr. Herbert P. *Fort Victoria, from Fur Trading Post to Capital City of B.C.*. Illustrated booklet: no publishing information, ND

Smith, Dorothy Blakey, ed. *The Reminiscences of Doctor John Sebastian Helmcken.* Vancouver: University of British Columbia Press, 1975

Turner, Robert. *Vancouver Island Railways.* San Marino, CA: Golden West Books, 1973

Victoria Historical Review. Victoria Centennial Celebration Society. 1962

Victoria, the Queen City, published "under the auspices of the Corporation of the City of Victoria." 1891

Virgin, Victor. *History of North and South Saanich*. Victoria: 1978

Walbran, Captain John T. *British Columbia Coast Names*: Ottawa: Government Printing Bureau, 1909. (Vancouver Public Library reprint, 1971)

Index